or less innocent adventure. But the adventure has, indeed, become a very serious one. You have perfectly entranced one, I am carried off my feet, and cannot reach ground any longer. When I try to rehearse how it all happened, I cannot quite remember, but I do remember how wonderfully sweet you were, how willingly you kissed me, how sweetly you gave yourself without resisting, though you had said that you were not certain that you approved of lovers.

Oh my darling, what incredible happiness it is, and how madly I love you.

T.

To Susan, my Beloved

BOOKS BY BRENDA UELAND

If You Want to Write

Me: A Memoir

Strength to Your Sword Arm: Selected Writings

Mitropoulos and the North High Band

O Clouds Unfold! Clara Ueland and her Family

✳

BOOKS BY FRIDTJOF NANSEN

The First Crossing of Greenland

Eskimo Life

Farthest North: The Voyage and Exploration of the Fram, 1893-96

Norway and the Union with Sweden

In Northern Mists: Arctic Exploration in Early Times

Through Siberia: The Land of the Future

Sporting Days in Wild Norway

Russia and Peace

Adventure, and other papers

Armenia and the Near East

Through the Caucasus to the Volga

To Patty, My Darling, or Something Sweet. Happy Birthday! "True love til the end of Time!" Love Gary

BRENDA
MY DARLING

THE LOVE LETTERS
OF FRIDTJOF NANSEN TO BRENDA UELAND

Eric Utne 11/22/11

EDITED BY
ERIC UTNE

WITH A FOREWORD BY
PER EGIL HEGGE

An UTNE Institute Book, October 2011

Copyright © 2011 by Eric Utne

Published in the United States by the UTNE Institute, Inc., a 501c3
public charitable organization, with offices at 4259 Linden Hills Blvd.,
Minneapolis, Minnesota 55410 USA.

Portions of this book have appeared elsewhere. Grateful acknowledgment
is made to the Schubert Club and the Estate of Brenda Ueland for
permission to reprint previously published material.

Library of Congress Control Number: 2011913430
BRENDA, MY DARLING:
The Love Letters of Fridtjof Nansen to Brenda Ueland

Edited by Eric Utne
Book design by Emily Utne
www.utneinstitute.org

ISBN 978-0-9761989-3-2

1. Nansen, Fridtjof. 2. Ueland, Brenda. 3. Utne, Eric. 4. Letters—Literary
Collections. 5. Personal Memoirs—United States—Biography.
6. Adventurers & Explorers—Biography.
7. Women—United States—Biography. 8. New York (N.Y.)—Biography.

Printed in Canada
10 9 8 7 6 5 4 3 2 1

CONTENTS

FOREWORD

IT IS NO EXAGGERATION to say that these love letters from Fridtjof Nansen to Brenda Ueland make for compelling reading. Nansen's fiery confessions of his great love for Ueland would have been considered semi-pornographic only a half century ago. The Norwegian saying "when the old house catches fire, it burns with great heat," fully applies. But, because the letters are so earnest, so intense, and so beautifully written, it is more appropriate to classify them as literature—a true love song.

Nansen's English is poetic and aesthetic, but then he had 40 years of practice. As a young man he taught himself to quote long passages of Byron and Keats by heart. Moreover, he had been on several speaking tours in the United Kingdom and the United States, where he lectured about his adventures skiing across Greenland and his voyage over the Arctic Ocean, from the pulpit of the Royal Geographical Society in London.

What is most remarkable about these letters is how Nansen opens up and exposes himself for Ueland, who was younger than him by 30 years. The aloof and taciturn aristocrat we have come to know from his other writing is rarely seen in these letters.

Fridtjof Nansen's strong interest in the other sex, and his appeal to the same, was never a secret, including for his immediate family. One could say he earned his reputation as a lover of women. In fact it was a strain in his marriage to Eva Sars. In December 1907 Nansen was in London, where he was in the process of completing his assignment as a diplomat. Preparing to return home to Norway, he received news that Eva had suddenly become seriously ill. He left immediately, but he did not reach her deathbed in time. Eva Nansen died at the age of 49. He regretted the suffering he caused Eva for the rest of his life.

Fridtjof Nansen was one of the first Norwegians interested in Sigmund Freud's scientific work. There are five references to Freud in Nansen's doctoral thesis. Freud was occupied at the time not with human mental life, but with liver cancer and diseases of the nervous system. But both men realized early—with completely different paths for their own careers—the role of eroticism and sexuality in human emotions.

Brenda Ueland (1891-1985) and Fridtjof Nansen (1861-1930) first met in 1929. Nansen was in the U.S. on what would be his last U.S. visit. Brenda wrote to him as a freelance journalist requesting an interview. But she admits that it was a pretext. She was more curious about the person than the interview. As Ueland's grandson Eric Utne writes in this book's Introduction, their mutual interest must have turned into an immediate attraction, quickly becoming an almost unmanageable infatuation.

In the brief period they were together in New York City and Connecticut, there may not have been many opportunities to pursue their attraction. Their correspondence began immediately after his return to Norway. She could sit for five hours at a time writing letters to him. He told her that he did not think about anything, and certainly no one, other than her. He held little back when he described his erotic obsession with her. He became upset when too much time passed between letters—that is to say more than two weeks.

As usual, he was careful to be discreet. He told her to send her letters in envelopes that appeared to be official, and to be sure that the name and address were typed rather than written by hand.

In these letters Nansen revealed to Ueland something about his past relationships that none of his many biographers seems to have discovered: that he and Marie Holdt were lovers. Mrs. Holdt, married to Pastor William Holdt, was Nansen's much older hostess when the young scientist lived in Bergen from 1882-1888. Fifteen years his senior, she took care of more of her young tenant's needs than you can reasonably expect of a landlord. Of this relationship he writes poetically, gently, and beautifully.

As an old woman, Brenda Ueland gave a brisk interview to Erik Bye on NRK, the Norwegian equivalent of PBS. She said, "I'm so old they'll need to shoot me on Judgment Day." She was 93 years, and was both fresh and discreet about the past. She could have brought her secret to the grave, except for the hints in her autobiography. But she did not burn his letters. Over 80 years after they were written, these letters take us far from the mists and glaciers of Nansen's Arctic adventures. They give us the opportunity to admire the literary Fridtjof Nansen and to savor the heart-felt expression of his poetic soul.

So burning are these letters that one is tempted to recall a bit of 1 Corinthians. "Three things will last forever—faith, hope, and love—and the greatest of these is love."

Per Egil Hegge
September 2011
Oslo, Norway

"I am so glad that you liked my little drawing...
of course I thought of you when I drew it."

—F.N., February 28, 1930

x

INTRODUCTION

*

"Listen to the reed and the tale it tells,
How it sings of separation..."
–RUMI

"You cannot possibly understand what your letter means to me, it is as
if a flood of strength suffuses my whole body and soul, and I feel that
you are near... What an irresistible attraction towards you, what a warm
feeling of tenderness, also because you wish me to know you exactly as
you are. And I feel the same desire; there is not a corner of my heart or
soul which I do not wish you to look into...simply because it is all parts of
my own self, and you have to know it. I have a feeling that I could talk to
you about everything, as I have <u>never</u> had before, and you would always
understand..."
—FRIDTJOF NANSEN TO BRENDA UELAND, 25 APRIL 1929

P assion may be greatest when there are great obstacles. In
the 12th century, Heloise, forcibly separated from her much
older lover Abelard, wrote to him, "While I am denied
your presence, give me at least through your words some sweet
semblance of yourself." So too with Rumi's 13th-century poems of
longing for his beloved Shams of Tabriz, and Elizabeth Barrett's
tender correspondence with Robert Browning ["Sonnets from
the Portuguese" (1847)]; separation breeds passion, creativity,
and the power of the imagination.

This book is the record of another such literary love affair,

1

one that took place in the 20th century, reached across a vast ocean, and spanned a thirty-year age difference. The letters from Fridtjof Nansen to Brenda Ueland are evidence that two questing souls found each other, and, through an intense, clandestine correspondence, transformed each other's lives. Promising absolute honesty, they practiced uncommon candor. They revealed their innermost thoughts, and swore never to destroy, censor, or even withhold anything they'd written from the other. Thus, they inspired each other's most passionate and eloquent thoughts, their very best selves.

Readers will find here only half of Nansen and Ueland's year-long correspondence. Unfortunately, Ueland's letters to Nansen, which must have been absolutely incendiary, were probably burned by his son Odd and daughter-in-law Kari when they found them after Nansen's death. Fortunately, Ueland was a gifted and prolific writer. You will learn why Nansen was so besotted with her, through selections from her published works and heretofore unpublished diaries.

Brenda Ueland and Fridtjof Nansen met in early 1929, when she was 37, he 67. She was a free-lance writer and single mother living in Stamford, Connecticut, and working in New York City. He was a world-famous explorer, statesman, and humanitarian preparing for his next Arctic expedition. They had a brief love affair—just a few days spent together in New York and Stamford, followed by a year-long correspondence that lasted until shortly before Nansen's death on May 13, 1930.

This is a true love story, as poignant and fraught with intrigue and anguish as that of Tristan and Isolde, or Abelard and Heloise. Like theirs, it is a literary love affair, played out at a distance. Fridtjof and Brenda, separated by the Atlantic Ocean and a three-decade age difference, came to know each other and consummated their passions primarily in their imaginations.

BRENDA UELAND was born October 24, 1891, in Minneapolis, Minnesota. Her grandfather, Ole Gabriel Ueland, was a farmer and statesman who served in the first Norwegian Storting (parliament). Her father, Andreas Ueland, immigrated to the U.S. as a child, dug sewers as a young man, and eventually prospered as a lawyer and judge. Her mother, Clara Ueland, was a prominent, civic-minded suffragette and progressive parent who gave her seven children great freedom. "My parents were political idealists, feminists, democrats," Brenda wrote. "They wanted their children to be light-hearted and athletic, to live outdoors and eat oranges and apples. My mother thought the girls should not be the menials of the boys, and so the boys made their own beds and the girls were on the football team in the pasture. She thought that if mothers were what they should be, surrounding their children with every freedom and happiness and cheerful intelligence, we would have the Millennium in one generation. She taught the baby how to hold and smooth the cat. She never cautioned us. We could walk endless miles in the country, swim across the lake, ride bareback."

Brenda attended Wells College in upstate New York and Barnard College in New York City. Living in Greenwich Village she traveled with such bohemian free thinkers and literary lions as Mabel Dodge, Emma Goldman, Theodore Dreiser, Willa Cather, Eugene O'Neill, and John Reed. She married in 1916, had a daughter, Gabriel [Gaby], in 1921, and was divorced in 1926. In the 1930s Brenda wrote her two best-known books, *If You Want to Write* (1938) and *Me* (1939), both published by G.P. Putnam's Sons.

If You Want to Write begins, "Everybody is talented, original, and has something important to say..." and Brenda believed it. When the book came out an incredulous *Saturday Review of Literature* reviewer attacked Brenda's idea that most people should write. "Let the mediocre stick to reading," he advised. Don't offer "false hopes to the untalented." Pulitzer Prize-winning poet and biographer Carl Sandburg thought otherwise. He called *If You Want to Write* "the best book ever written about how to write." (As of this writing the book has sold more than 300,000 copies since 1987, with a devoted following.)

The next year G.P. Putnam's Sons published *Me*, the story of the first half of Brenda's self-described "very unconventional life." In an edition re-issued in 1993, memoirist Patricia Hampl wrote that Brenda was a true "rule-breaking woman," and that *Me* was her "masterpiece."

In the 1940s Brenda wrote a column for the *Minneapolis Times*, and in 1945 received Norway's highest honor, the Knights of St. Olaf medal, for her coverage of Vidkun Quisling's trial and her relief work after World War II. She corresponded with, and was admired by, Langston Hughes, Paul Robeson, Eleanor Roosevelt, Upton Sinclair, Robert Penn Warren, and Carl Sandburg, among countless others.

During the last three decades of her life Brenda lived in a small, wood-frame house near Lake Harriet, a lovely, spring-fed urban lake whose forested public shoreline held park-like trails. She walked the lake twice a day, "Once for the body and once for the soul." She was recognized around the city for her frequent, meandering 20-mile walks. "It is much better to walk alone," she wrote, "no cackle of voices at your elbow to jar the meditative silence of the morning."

Toward the end of her long life, with her typical tongue-in-cheek braggadocio, Brenda told me she had "three husbands and a hundred lovers." But, she added, striving never to be dishonest or cruel, she "tried not to have a love affair with a married man unless he brought a note from his wife." She got one once. It said, "You can have him!"

Brenda's true love was life itself. "While you are alive, be *alive!*" was one of her favorite maxims. She had little patience for those who merely endured life rather than celebrating it. Her days were filled with passionate curiosity and conversation—about Tolstoy, Blake, Joan of Arc, railroad bums, marching bands, courage, and beauty. These were also the subjects of her writing.

She worked in her sunny, second floor studio, looking out over the lake, "Like Captain Ahab, watching the whales spouting," she said. She wrote for local periodicals, lectured widely, and kept extensive diaries.

She took in stray cats and stray people with regularity. She set three AAU swimming records in the over-80 category, "because it took me longer to sink than the competition." She maintained the house herself, changing her heavy storm windows atop a stepladder well into her 80s. At 90, she fell from the ladder and broke her hip. She said the worst part of it was that she could no longer "dart from in between parked cars in the middle of city blocks and dodge on-coming traffic."

Brenda wrote every day—short stories, essays, newspaper columns, a journal, serials—by her estimate over six million published words. In her later years she became mentor and advisor to a circle of young writers. She would tell them stories of her life, if asked, but mostly she would listen, asking many questions of her young friends. "If you want to be interesting," she'd admonish them, "you have to be interested." She was interested in everything—politics, natural foods, beauty, bravery, protecting defenseless animals, and the Minnesota Vikings football team.

Brenda's secret for healthy living was the same as for good writing—slow down, as in, "long, inefficient, happy idling, dawdling and puttering." And this: "...inspiration does not come like a bolt, nor is it kinetic, energetic striving, but it comes slowly and quietly and all the time, though we must regularly and every day give it a little chance to start flowing; prime it with a little solitude and idleness... you should feel when writing not like Lord Byron on a mountaintop, but like a child stringing beads in kindergarten—happy, absorbed, and quietly putting one bead on after another."

Even as she unfailingly encouraged others, she mercilessly criticized herself. She wrote in her diary in 1958:

> I remembered this morning to be WHOLE, to not suppress any of many manifold personalities—the seventeen wrapped into one. Sainthood commingled with Satanic-hood—it is this that leads to illumination and mental aliveness...I am physically NOT as fine as I should be—stiff, and thick through the waist. I have been trying to correct this PHYSICALLY—by more exercise, walking, better food etc. But I have neglected the

spirit, imagination, laboring travailing mind and spirit. THIS one gets only by writing, I think, for hours, hours every day. I am sure of it. I see it suddenly now, and clearly. I have seen it intermittently for many years, but have forgotten it again.

౮ౚ *A Love Story* ౚ౮

OUR LOVE STORY begins in 1928. Brenda described it in her autobiography *Me*:

Now I come to a love story. In 1928 my father went to Norway and wanted me to go; but I was too anxious about making a living. He wanted to take care of all that, but there was my old complex about not being an expense, a nuisance. Besides, freelancing is not like a salaried job. The work you do this month may not be paid for, for six months or two years, or ever. So I was dogged by conscientiousness. And all the time living expenses, rent and so on, went right on ticking off hundreds of dollars, like a kind of relentless gas meter.

So I would not go. But I saw Father off on the boat and felt sorry about it, and sorrier later, because on this boat he got to know Fridtjof Nansen, the Arctic explorer. He was the great man of Norway. As well as an explorer, he was a famous scientist, a zoologist and oceanographer; he had been ambassador to London during the critical period of disunion from Sweden in 1905; and as the representative of Norway to the League of Nations, it was he who had repatriated millions of prisoners of war.

That winter Nansen came to this country [the U.S.]. I read it in the newspaper. He was planning, it said, to go with Eckener in the Graf Zeppelin across the North Pole, and he had come to make arrangements with the United States government, for mooring masts in Alaska.

I wrote him a note and asked for an interview. I did not

really want the interview so much as to see him and to talk to him. This was my hero-worship. I felt that he was really great. If I could just get near and see him and hear him talk a little. In answer, he wrote me that he must go west but after that, when he returned to New York in March, he would surely see me...

For a year we wrote each other every week, until his death. We had a plan that when he came the next spring to go in the airship across the Pole, I would go with him. He would arrange it...

I was so much in love with him that it was hard to keep from writing to him all the time. I could easily spend five rapt, vanishing hours on a single letter. And a letter from him was the light of my days, and I have never in my life felt just this way at any time. The most disconnected things would sing through me like music, just looking out on a spring morning, toward the Sound, toward the poplar tree and the tangled ragged meadow of gorse. The words: "Whose name is writ in water" went across my mind, and such a strange and unconnected thought like that, but it struck me and sang through me and made gold harp wires of me. Those words and something vague about Keats would make tears of inexplicable rapture come into my eyes.

Of course when I think of my letters to him, I have my usual dislike for myself of yesterday, because they were so planned, so composed. I wrote them over and over, as though they were poems. That wish to be effective—I am always so afraid there is insincerity in it. Yet I did love him unutterably and there has never been anything like it.

And all the time, you understand, it was a sort of dream love affair, a literary one. We never really believed we would see each other (again). And yet I know my letters were comforting and exciting to him. I can tell from his. And I am so glad they were.

FRIDTJOF NANSEN was possibly the first truly global citizen, one of the best-known explorers and most popular personalities of his day. He is still Norway's favorite son. He earned his fame in 1888 as the first person to cross Greenland on skis. In 1895, he got closer to the North Pole than anyone before him. An oceanographer, he observed a current in the far North previously undetected. That discovery led to his audacious idea to build a sturdy, round-hulled, crush-resistant ship, the Fram, and deliberately freeze it into the Arctic ice floe. For more than a year and a half he and his crew of twelve men drifted until they were close enough for Nansen to make a dash for the pole with one other man and a team of twenty-eight sled dogs. The "dash," planned to take three months, took fifteen and the entire journey more than three years. Nansen's daring feat won him world fame and universal admiration. He was a noted zoologist and a pioneer of neuron theory. He was also a distinguished diplomat and humanitarian, eventually becoming High Commissioner of Refugees for the League of Nations, for which he won the Nobel Peace Prize in 1922. The Nobel Peace Prize Institute describes Nansen's humanitarian work:

> In the spring of 1920, the League of Nations asked Nansen to undertake the task of repatriating the prisoners of war, many of them held in Russia. Moving with his customary boldness and ingenuity, and despite restricted funds, Nansen repatriated 450,000 prisoners in the next year and a half.
>
> In June, 1921, the Council of the League, spurred by the International Red Cross and other organizations, instituted its High Commission for Refugees and asked Nansen to administer it. For the stateless refugees under his care Nansen invented the "Nansen Passport," a document of identification which was eventually recognized by fifty-two governments...
>
> The Red Cross in 1921 asked Nansen to take on yet a third humanitarian task, that of directing relief for millions

of Russians dying in the famine of 1921-1922. Help for Russia, then suspect in the eyes of most of the Western nations, was hard to muster, but Nansen pursued his task with awesome energy. In the end he gathered and distributed enough supplies to save a staggering number of people, the figures quoted ranging from 7,000,000 to 22,000,000.

In 1922 at the request of the Greek government and with the approval of the League of Nations, Nansen tried to solve the problem of the Greek refugees who poured into their native land from their homes in Asia Minor after the Greek army had been defeated by the Turks. Nansen arranged an exchange of about 1,250,000 Greeks living on Turkish soil for about 500,000 Turks living in Greece, with appropriate indemnification and provisions for giving them the opportunity for a new start in life.

Nansen's fifth great humanitarian effort, at the invitation of the League in 1925, was to save the remnants of the Armenian people from extinction. He drew up a political, industrial, and financial plan for creating a national home for the Armenians in Erivan that foreshadowed what the United Nations Technical Assistance Board and the International Bank of Development and Reconstruction have done in the post-World War II period. The League failed to implement the plan, but the Nansen International Office for Refugees later settled some 10,000 in Erivan and 40,000 in Syria and Lebanon.

⌁ A Tortured, Restless Dreamer ⌁

DR. GRO HARLEM BRUNDTLAND, the former Prime Minister of Norway, described Nansen as a "tortured, restless dreamer":

This description of Nansen may come as a surprise to many. Steely determination, will power, and almost superhuman perseverance are the characteristics for which he is best

9

known. And rightly so. These are the qualities which got him across Greenland on skis, brought him next to the North Pole, and made him survive the harsh Arctic winters.

But there is no contradiction here. It is hardly an original observation that greatness only occurs when passion and reason meet. Often this encounter leads to violent clashes, torturing the poor soul who has to balance his intense desires with his sense of duty and discipline.

These clashes are so evident in Nansen, who despite his great exploits rarely seemed at peace, and who—we may observe—was never able to fully enjoy his own achievements. Nansen, it seemed, always wanted to be somewhere else, with someone else, and doing something else. Yet, he always completed what he set as tasks for himself, and he did them brilliantly.

A fundamental element in understanding his achievements is to realize how he—despite his continuous internal battles— was able throughout his life to combine passion with reason and harness the energy this fusion created to do great things.

Through his work as researcher and explorer, and his path-setting humanitarian work after the First World War, he mobilized fellow citizens and world opinion. In surmounting obstacles and sometimes bursting conventions, he led the way to actions in humanitarian assistance, which have become a national pride to his own country and an inspiration for other people and nations. He developed ways to assist women, men, and children in need, and he bore the torch for human rights, long before they were put down on paper as we know them today.

Through all this he helped politicians to realize that "charity is Realpolitik," as Nansen put it. When all is said and done, this may be his greatest humanitarian legacy...Sergei Rachmaninoff, Igor Stravinsky, and Marc Chagall could all testify to this. They were among the many who were given new legitimacy with the "Nansen Passport," an identity document guaranteed by the League of Nations that gave these Russian refugees a legal status and allowed them to travel freely.

Fridtjof Nansen knew the urgency of an emergency. One tale from his arctic adventures is frequently told to young generations of Norwegians. Nansen had nearly reached the North Pole with his companion Hjalmar Johansen... [when] they had to turn around to head towards the mainland farther south.

Since they had to cross open stretches of water, the two men [used] their kayaks. As they prepared to enter their small unstable boats, Hjalmar Johansen was attacked by a huge polar bear. The bear threw the man onto the ice. Johansen, known for his incredible strength, stretched his arms and held on to the cheeks of the bear. Nansen, in the meantime, desperately reached for his gun, which he had already placed in his kayak. But the boat slipped away and the great explorer had to struggle to get hold of his kayak and his rifle.

Johansen, looking into the terrifying teeth of the polar bear, could hardly hold on for much longer, but he kept his calm and respectfully spoke these famous words to his patron:

'Sir, I do believe you need to hurry up—if not it will be too late.'

Nansen finally did get hold of his rifle and shot the bear.

We too need to hurry. The life and the efforts of Fridtjof Nansen provide us with the inspiration to strive for human progress, dignity, and development—for this generation and those to come.

☙ Quisling Karma ❧

VIDKUN QUISLING played a strangely significant role for both Nansen and Ueland. During the 1920s Quisling was Nansen's trusted assistant and representative to his famine relief work in the Ukraine. He was also Nansen's delegate in his attempts to defend the remaining Armenian people after the genocide in Turkey in 1915-1922. By all accounts Quisling was an able, tireless man, fluent in Russian and, in Nansen's words, an "absolutely indispensable" envoy. But fifteen years later Quisling's name would become infamous as the arch-collaborator and traitor during the Nazi occupation of Norway. He was tried and executed for treason in 1945. His name is now a noun, defined as, "a person who betrays his or her own country by aiding an invading enemy, often serving later in a puppet government."

Brenda traveled to Norway to cover the Quisling trial that summer. In one of her columns for the *Minneapolis Times*, dated August 22, 1945, she wrote:

> At Quisling's trial he was brought in by two unsmiling young soldiers. Everybody rose quietly to gaze at him. He is a big man with an extraordinary flabby white and blotched face. His eyes, under puffed lids, have dark glittering surface glare, not unlike Hitler's.
>
> The Norwegian spirit is remarkable. On the surface, in judges, audience, people outside on the street, there is a quiet, searching conscientiousness to know the truth, to be fair.
>
> But underneath one can sense how this man has caused continuous terror, anguish to every family in Norway for five years.
>
> There are four judges and five jurymen sitting in now like our supreme court, and the trial is more informal than ours, less held up with legal technique. One feels there is a more simple search into truth.
>
> Quisling stands up often to say he was saving Norway from England, that documents captured in Berlin aren't true, and he and the judge talk back and forth in their mild harmless-sounding Norwegian inflection.
>
> Quisling in power ranted like Hitler, now he is humble,

horribly beseeching. You feel he is making an agonized effort
to save his life.

Brenda was awarded the St. Olaf Medal by Norway's King Haakon VII
for, "commendable spreading of knowledge about Norway abroad,
and for promoting connections and solidarity between emigrated
Norwegians and the homeland." Years later she joked that she'd been
"knighted by the king of Norway." Asked if she told the king at her
award ceremony that she was descended from Norway's King Sverre,
circa 1150 AD, Brenda replied, "No, I didn't mention King Sverre
because I didn't want King Haakon to feel uncomfortable. He might
feel I thought he was only a pretender and not in the direct line."

✐ *"He talked always about you to me"* ✐

IN 1938, eight years after Nansen's death, Brenda received a letter
from Kari, his daughter-in-law. Kari wrote, "…I am sure I will make
you happy by sending you this letter from F.N.—I found it here by
his papers just after his death—but I could not send it without your
address—and for 8 years I have been still hoping you would give me a
"sign" sometime.… I have always understood that you were in love with
each other—and here at home some lovely pictures were found too [of
Brenda] but we put them to fire because we were afraid some people
could find them, who would not understand. I love you because I feel
so well that you had the right feelings about him—and he talked always
about you to me.…"

✐ *Two Seekers After Wisdom* ✐

IN 1926, Nansen was inaugurated as Lord Rector of St. Andrews
University, Scotland, joining the ranks of previous honorees Rudyard
Kipling and J.M. Barrie. In his address, titled "Adventure," he told the

students, "You will find your adventure, for life itself is an adventure.... The first thing to do is to find yourself. And for that you need solitude and contemplation...deliverance will come not from the rushing, noisy centers of civilization. It will come from the lonely places. The great reformers in history have come from the wilderness.... True wisdom is found far from men, out in the great solitude, and can only be attained through suffering. Privation and suffering are the only road to wisdom...."

In his remarkable quest for wisdom, Nansen personifies a 20th century Odin, king of the Norse gods—god of war, wisdom, poetry and magic. In one of his manifestations, Odin is called Vegtam, the Wanderer, traversing the world seeking wisdom so intently he gives up an eye to attain it.

Brenda Ueland personifies a 20th-century Freya, the Norse goddess associated with love, beauty, fertility, magic, prophecy and death—the most beloved, honored, and renowned among the Norse goddesses. Brenda too was renowned. Hundreds of thousands have been inspired by Brenda's book *If You Want to Write*. Like Freya, (and Shakespeare's Sylvia), Brenda was "holy, fair, and wise." And a mystic. In the introduction to her book, *Beauty and Bravery* [unpublished], Brenda sounds positively Freya-like:

> The word "health" also means "whole" and "holy." And you
> cannot have beauty and bravery and grandeur and exuberance,
> generosity and joviality and a kind of affectionate fearlessness
> unless you have health. Nor indeed can you be really sane.

Odin and Freya were both married to others—Odin's wives were Frigg and Jodd (the Earth), and Freya's husband was Odr. Yet Odin and Freya were really meant for each other—they were true partners and natural soul mates. These letters from Fridtjof Nansen to Brenda Ueland are the letters Odin would have written to Freya.

❧ *"Ah well, we are all complex"* ❧

BECAUSE BRENDA'S letters to Nansen were lost or perhaps "put to fire," we turn to Brenda's diaries to learn her thoughts at the time of their correspondence. Until reading these diaries, in a restricted section of the archives of the Minnesota Historical Society, I thought Brenda was kidding me when she claimed she'd had "three husbands and a hundred lovers." Now I believe her. During the roughly twelve months that Ueland and Nansen corresponded (April 1929-April 1930), Brenda was involved in a number of intimate relationships, with both men and women, including the author and fashion illustrator Grace Hart, whom Brenda refers to only as Tomola. When Brenda met Nansen, in March 1929, she had been married once, to William Benedict from 1916-1926, and in 1921 had given birth to Gaby, her only child. After Nansen, Brenda would marry twice more: Manus McFadden, editor of the *Minneapolis Times*, followed by Norwegian American artist Sverre Hanssen.

The only surviving letter from Brenda to Nansen that has been found is the following abridged letter she entered into her diary Monday, February 24th 1930:

> Darling Fridtjof,
> I have been working very hard and this is not just the usual protest of one who has been soldiering, malingering (which is usually so in my case), but I have sworn to write an article in two weeks, instead of taking the usual five or six...
> Today I am kind of tired, not enough sleep and too much work. But it is a glorious day with thick yellow sun drowning the earth and it is as warm as May and so it has been for three or four days, so that I go walking without stockings or sleeves and have already a thin, mottled, jaundiced looking tan. I have so much to tell you. I ought to tell you everything, but there is so much. That is the trouble with writing so infrequently, if one could only write every day, one could write many pages.

15

But when it is put off there is too much to tell and so it only becomes a bleak resume. But now I will see what I can get said.

I feel quiet and because inevitably our vigorous interest in each other must wane a little, though this is only because of discouragement and because there is no certain possibility of seeing each other. But if only the definite possibility turned up, say I heard you were coming to this country, six months from now, why my feelings would be revived in all their fierceness. I wish you were coming...

There is a man in love with me now and I have experimented with a love affair again; a nice, nice honorable manly fellow whose wife is away in Florida and who does not love him at all though he is too simple and honest to be aware of this. She leaves him for six months every year and then he must live alone in a boarding house in Bridgeport and his company is failing and carrying down in its crash all his money. (His wife has money of her own.) So I have been very good to him, make him come down here for dinner, got him to fall in love with me. You once said that in your case, flirtations and so on were due to the explorer in you and this is true in my case also...Ah well, we are all complex...

⸙ *"Do not forget your lonely Viking"* ⸙

WE PROBABLY will never find any more of what Brenda wrote to him than this, but Nansen's letters to her reveal much about each of them. He comes across as a man revitalized and opened wide. He writes to her, "...there is not a corner of my heart or soul which I do not wish you to look into – not because I think that there may not be much which is ungraceful or offensive, but simply because it is all parts of my own self, and you have to know it. I have a feeling that I could talk to you about everything, as I have never had before, and you would always understand."

16

In these letters Nansen shares with Brenda his sexual philosophy and history, including the details of a long affair he had with Marie Holdt, wife of Lutheran Pastor Wilhelm Holdt while Nansen lived with them in their Bergen home from 1882-1888. Most of Nansen's previous biographers have chosen not to disclose this affair, or had not discovered it.

Nansen told Brenda her letters gave him "new life, new vigor, new vitality…your 'wildness' is just like a refreshing bath in the fountain of life…it was as if my whole interior opened and absorbed your whole beautiful being, and I felt that really we belonged to each other, that you possessed me, and I had no desire to be free again."

In a letter dated May 23rd, 1929 he told Brenda:

You are a sorceress, indeed, you have tied me hand and foot, soul and body, everything, I am lost…you have perfectly entranced me, I am carried off my feet, and cannot reach ground any longer.

On June 2nd, 1929 he wrote:

You say you have "a longing for exploring, wandering over the world on its loneliest and saddest rims," O, if only we could wander together, my darling, what would it not be, what wonderful happiness, and what great things could we not do when we could complete each other! And you wish to go with me on the north polar expedition, dear darling, I feel like you, I…would not mind what happened as long as we two were together, the end has to come once anyhow…

…O yes, the future is unknown, happily, and so many things may happen, and it is no good to despair, and I will have hope and confidence, that something good and beautiful is still in store.

On June 19th, 1929 he confided to her his sense of isolation:

…Here at home I always lived the life of a hermit, working in my tower and never seeing anybody, a most unsociable and impossible man, whom now at last people as a rule leave alone, as he is known to be inaccessible.

Later, his letters began to reveal the waning of his life force, and a sense of regret. On July 7th he wrote:

...You are young, I am old, have you really considered how old I am? And how many years I have left?...When I look back upon life it is really strange, what I most regret and repent are the lost opportunities when the body, the instincts, the "flesh" was willing and courageous enough, but the brain cowardly held back, and the opportunity was not grasped.

And on July 19th, 1929:

...I think, that a man is not complete without the woman. There is an empty space in my soul, a void, it craves you, come fill it...Come let me feel that life is not ebbing out, passing away slowly, and nothing worth having is achieved. Come let me see that the real things, the worthy things, the things worth doing, can still be done...

On July 30th, 1929:

...I have just been writing about the brave Mohammedan mountain tribes in the Caucasus. They fought for victory or death. Victory meant liberty, death meant Paradise. And there were the Houris [beautiful, gazelle-eyed virgins awaiting Jihadi martyrs in Muslim paradise], smiling to them with black eyes like sparkling stars and arms like swan's necks. But not everybody will they embrace, only the brave ones. Fancy if you were the Houri, waiting for me, how I would fight, and how I would seek the most exposed places, to get to you as soon as possible across the bridge Al-Sirat. And when I succeeded, and the right bullet found me, how you would receive me on the other side of the bridge, and we would never, never more be separated in all eternity. I love you my dear darling, my mistress, my every thing, and wish I were in your arms.

Goodbye and do not forget your lonely Viking.

On November 28th, 1929 he wrote:

I am sorry that you have got a letter from me making you think that I am so very depressed and "empty." Yes I was, but don't worry darling, it never lasts so very long with me, a few days rest in the woods and I am alright again…

On December 14th, in his next letter:

Oh, my dear, dear girl how I long for you. So many, many things I wished to say, so many things to talk about, just to dive into your dear soul with all my thoughts, find rest and kindred thoughts, intermingle, just be ourselves and nothing else, far, far, far away from this restless, empty, worrying, tiresome, disgusting life, which I really loathe, and still have to go through and try to make the best of, and it gives no peace, always more than one can overcome. But I won't think of it now…

On January 20th, 1930 he wrote:

…Fancy this is actually the first letter I write to you in the New Year. I send you all good wishes for it, and do hope we may meet soon, it seems a whole lifetime since we parted, and this life is really absurd…I love you more than any words can express and wish that I could be with you in your nice quiet home and be your boy and your Viking.

A sense of foreboding pervades his letter dated February 28th, 1930:

…There has been so much disturbance lately, and I have been perfectly unfit for writing, and so I am still. I cannot say exactly what is the matter with me, but my brain seems so empty and will not work, and I miss you sadly, and still I cannot write a letter. Oh if only you were here with me, it would be all right at once. I must send you a few lines though to let you know that I am still alive, and long for you more than words can express, and hope soon to hear from you again, perhaps that will rouse my sleeping brain again.

…I am so glad that you liked my little drawing [see page x] with the New Year greeting. Of course I thought of you when I drew it …

Oh what an eternity it really is since I saw you, and how I miss you, and how much I need you I cannot tell you, and I do believe that you need me too, though you may find plenty of others over there. But do not forget me, please! I hope that soon I will be able to write you a real, nice letter, and that you will have patience with me, for you know I love you my dear girl and darling, and I long for a letter from you soon.

Your Viking Fridtjof

Then, on March 7th, 1930, in his penultimate letter to Brenda, he wrote:
Dear Brenda, my darling,
I am more sorry than I can say. I am tied to my bed for weeks and cannot write to you. I have suddenly quite unexpectedly and without any reason I know of got an attack of phlebitis in one leg, which is badly swollen, and have had to keep in bed without moving. The doctor says it is all right if only I do not move, but that is dangerous. How long I shall have to lie here I do not know, but it may take some weeks yet...

A thousand greetings. I wish you could be here, my dear, dear girl.

Fridtjof

On April 2nd, 1930 he wrote:
Brenda my darling,
I am so sorry. I am still lying here and cannot really write but will try to send you a few lines. Have been in bed for more than a month now and may have to remain there for three or four weeks more, so you must not expect any letter from me for some time yet. After I sent you a few lines I had a bad time:

suddenly got a blood clot in one lung, and it was a little serious. But I am all right now but must keep perfectly quiet on my back, and cannot do any work. It needs patience. How I wish you could have been here.

I got your letter where you mention your new l.a. [love affair]. So very, very nice of you to tell me all about it, and you know I understand perfectly. You certainly need it, you cannot live so lonely. Oh, how sad that there is such a distance between us, and that I do not know when we can meet. I also got your short letter with the film. I am so glad to have it. I wish I could do something really nice out of it. I think I could, if only I get the opportunity.

But now I cannot write more. Goodbye my darling, keep well and do not forget me. I love you and am your Viking.

Fridtjof

This was Nansen's last letter to Brenda. He died at his home, Polhøgda [Nansen's name for his house in Lysaker, outside Oslo. Polhøgda means "polar heights."], on May 13th, 1930, of a heart attack. He was given a state funeral on May 17th, Norway's Constitution (Independence) Day. His coffin, drawn by four black horses, like royalty, passed through Oslo's crowd-lined streets, and his ashes were placed under a tree at Polhøgda. He allowed no eulogies, only music. Schubert's "Death and the Maiden" rang somberly over the city.

✺ Eternal Womanhood Raises Us on High ✺

IN THE 1997 BIOGRAPHY *Nansen: The Explorer as Hero*, Roland Huntford writes in an epilogue:

Nansen…opened the era of modern polar exploration, the last chapter of terrestrial discovery, and inspired his successors, and his life encompassed its extent. He was one of the great

21

explorers of the Age of Discovery, which began with the Italian, Spanish, and Portuguese navigators of the fifteenth century and ended only with the attainment of the South Pole. With his wide attainments, he approached the Renaissance ideal of the universal man.

On (Nansen's) last visit to America, a journalist called Brenda Ueland made his acquaintance. She recorded in her diary:

When he says good-bye to me and kisses my hand, I shall never forget his face and I know that he loves me, for there is the terrible look of the sense-of-eternity or the sense-of-death in it. In the cab on the way to the train, he spoke one sentence of great sadness, 'I wonder if I will ever again...' Earlier in the evening...he speaks of 'Faust' (I cannot remember what he said).

Perhaps he had quoted to her the last lines of Goethe's tragedy:

Das Ewig-Wiebliche
Zeit uns hinan
'Eternal womanhood
Raises us on high.'

✒ "All Those Nice Souls Waiting Over Yonder" ✑

BRENDA ENTERED MY LIFE when I was 12 years old, when she married my grandfather, Sverre Hanssen, her third and last husband. As Brenda described it, her marriage to Sverre was "a conspiracy of fate to bring the two of us together," as she leaned forward to look conspiratorially into my eyes, our foreheads almost touching, "because you and I Eric, we're closer than kin."

Brenda was the most encouraging person I ever met, seemingly interested in everything I had to say, no matter how mundane. She made me feel fascinating, witty, and full of promise and even potential

22

greatness. She did the same for everyone around her.

She wrote this inscription to me in one of her books: "To my incomparably handsome grandson, so strangely full of lightheartedness and grandeur at the same time...There is a star on his forehead and his existence cheers up the world. I love him day and night and in the middle of the night." Who could resist such extravagant flattery? I didn't have a chance, and neither, clearly, did Nansen.

Brenda was clear and lucid and lively to the end. I lived a couple of blocks from her house to be close to her. She'd call me once or twice a week at about 5:00 PM and say, "Whatchya doin'?" which meant, "Come on down and have a Manhattan." If she'd sworn off liquor, as she frequently did, lamenting that it "stupefies the soul," we'd have peppermint tea.

Just weeks before she died, Brenda talked to me about the prospect of her death. "It's a joke," she said. "I can hardly wait. It's the biggest adventure I've had yet—all those nice souls waiting over yonder." On March 5th, 1985, at the age of 93, she set off to meet those souls. One of the eager ones waiting for her was surely her Odin, Fridtjof Nansen.

✒ *The Tendance of the Soul* ✑

IN HER ESSAY "On Making Choices," Brenda said that Plato believed the purpose of life is the "tendance of the soul...that is to say, we are in school. And like Plato," she wrote, "I believe in the Doctrine of Reminiscence or Reincarnation, and that in this life we are supposed to learn something, to advance, to become better. As in Ibsen's mystical drama, *Peer Gynt*, I think our soul, or Solveig, is waiting for us at the end of life and hopes that we have...learned something through striving, mistakes, suffering, and the like."

Two of the many things that Brenda learned in life were the power of listening and the importance of true equality between the sexes. In her essay "Tell Me More" Brenda writes:

Listening is a magnetic and strange thing, a creative force...

23

This is the reason: When we are listened to, it creates us, makes us unfold and expand. Ideas actually begin to grow within us and come to life...When we listen to people there is an alternating current, and this recharges us so that we never get tired of each other. We are constantly being re-created...[a] creative fountain inside us begins to spring and cast up new thoughts and unexpected laughter and wisdom...Now this little creative fountain is in all. It is the spirit, or the intelligence, or the imagination—whatever you want to call it...When people really listen to us, with quiet fascinated attention, the little fountain begins to work again, to accelerate in the most surprising way...

From their letters we can tell that Nansen and Brenda truly listened to each other. As Nansen wrote, ""I have a feeling that I could talk to you about everything, as I never had before, and you would always understand..."

Brenda's essay "The True, Little Known History of Women" reveals another reason why she and Nansen were so drawn to the other. In relation to each other, Brenda became a *real* woman and Nansen a *real* man. They were each other's archetypal equals. In the essay Brenda writes:

I want an honorable equality...[men and women] must have equal power in our society. Women want to foster life, not coerce and destroy it... Robert Graves says this: "A real woman" he says—he points out that the word "real" is the same word as "royal"—"A real woman neither despises nor worships men, but...knows the full extent of her powers and feels free to reject all arbitrary man-made obligations. She is her own oracle of right and wrong, firmly believing in her own five senses and the intuitive sixth...Since she never settles for the second best in love, what troubles her is the rareness of real men"...

Women have almost no friends among men—we are always loved for the wrong thing—only a few very great ones,

24

Pythagoras, Plato, Sophocles, Shakespeare, John Stuart Mill, Ibsen, Bernard Shaw. It seems to me one of the best ways to be a great man would be to be a true friend of women. You would be in good company. How? Neither pamper nor exploit them. Love in women their greatness, which is the same as it is in men. Insist on bravery, honor, grandeur, generosity in women...I say this because I think there is a state of great unhappiness between us. If we can be true equals, we will be better friends, better lovers, better wives and husbands.

These passages, and the hard-won life wisdom they embody, reveal the brilliant, path-breaking, visionary, generous-spirited, regal and real woman whom Nansen loved so intensely and well. Together, Brenda became the Divine Feminine, Nansen the Divine Masculine.

Brenda Ueland and Fridtjof Nansen were two questing souls who found each other, as truly resonant souls sometimes do. Each helped the other step out of a private darkness and into the light. Through lives of deep searching, they reached across oceans and generations to draw each other out. We can be glad they did, for their own sake, and for the written evidence of their love they left behind.

The eloquence, passion, and candor of these two extraordinary individuals serves as an inspiration to us all to tend our souls. The only way is through life experience, especially through struggling, in the crucible of life, to learn how to love. In this way we refine our souls, becoming more open, more transparent, more loving and luminous human beings. May we all find, as Brenda put it, "True love till the end of Time."

***

EDITOR'S NOTE

↷ *"Onward! Avanti! Fram!"* ↶

I DON'T REMEMBER when I first learned of Fridtjof Nansen's letters to Brenda Ueland. It may have been around the time that I joined the board of the Nobel Peace Prize Forum, in 2005, a cónsortium of five Midwest colleges with Norwegian roots that host an annual peace conference featuring the previous year's Peace Prize winner. After I read the letters it took me several years to decide to publish them. When you read them you will understand why. The letters are passionate. The question that nagged me was, "How would Brenda and Nansen feel about having their passion shared with the world?"

After immersing myself in Brenda's diaries and much sincere soul-searching, I felt clear that Brenda would approve. But what about Nansen? In 2006, I had the letters transcribed, and showed them to various family members and friends. Their response was invariably affirmative. "You must publish them," they said. "Would you hesitate if these were letters from Marc Antony to Cleopatra, Napoleon to Josephine?" Still, I had doubts.

The letters are extraordinarily eloquent and informative, but also quite explicit—"hot," as Nansen himself described them. I decided to ask Norwegian friends who admire Nansen and honor his legacy what they would recommend. One said, "You *must* publish the letters. They do not diminish a great man. On the contrary, they make him even greater, because they show a dimension of him we did not know. They make him more *human.*"

I then contacted several Norwegian diplomats and historians. Geir Lundestad, Ph.D., an historian and the Director of the Norwegian Nobel Institute, encouraged me to publish them. I got the same response from Steinar Bryn, Ph.D., Professor at the Nansen Humanistic Academy and leader of its Dialogue Project; Carl Emil Vogt, Ph.D.,

26

historian at the University of Oslo and author of a forthcoming book on Nansen's international and humanitarian work from 1920-1930; and Roland Huntford, author of the 2001 biography, *Nansen: The Explorer as Hero*. They became a chorus of encouragement.

Finally, I asked Brenda and Nansen directly. I made a dream pilgrimage to one of the earth's "loneliest and saddest rims," a remote outcropping of sparkling Arctic ice. I found them waiting for me, expectantly, arms around each other's shoulders and wrapped in a single, gigantic polar bear pelt. I called out, "May I have your blessings to share your love letters with the world?" Nodding enthusiastically and shouting in unison, they replied, *"Onward! Avanti! Fram!"*

> Eric Utne
> Spring Equinox, March 21, 2011
> Minneapolis, Minnesota

The following letters are slightly abridged due to sexual content. I have corrected Nansen's occasional misspellings and/or grammatical errors, if the correction served to avoid reader confusion or enhance clarity. For example, Nansen spelled the word "thigh" as "tigh," and he conflated "each other" as "eachother." Given the passionate connection of Brenda and Nansen, the latter mistake may have been deliberate.

THE LETTERS

*

December 20th, 1928

My Dear Mr. Ueland,

Hearty thanks for your very kind invitation to be your guest during my stay in Minneapolis. I would appreciate it very highly indeed, and I sincerely hope that nothing will prevent me. I write at once to my manager, Mr. William B. Feakins (Lecture and Concert Management, Times Building, New York), in whose [hands] I have placed myself for all arrangements, and I hope he has made no other arrangements for my visit to Minneapolis.

Looking very much forward to meet you again, and with my warmest wishes of the season,

Yours sincerely,

Fritj·f Nansen

29

February 5th, 1929

Brenda Ueland
Shippen Point
Stamford, Connecticut

Dear Mr. Nansen,

Thank you for your letter and if you do get a chance to see me, be sure and let me know.

I don't know whether you want publicity or not, but from the nature of your mission, it might be useful to you. I make my living by writing for magazines and so I might be able to contribute something useful to your mission.

But if it turns out that you are too busy, you are to pay no further attention to these requests. And so good luck.

Yours sincerely,

Brenda Ueland

❧ By the time Nansen and Ueland met, in late March, 1929, Nansen had outlived almost all the great figures of the classic age of polar exploration. Shackleton and Peary had died some years before...Nansen was now a patently sick, unhappy man, suffering from cataracts and trapped in a miserable marriage.... For the first few months of 1929 he was in the United States, alone, on a lecture tour.... Still trying to raise money for his Arctic airship flight, he received little encouragement, and returned home April 6th.... Shortly before his departure Nansen meets Brenda Ueland at the home of Mr. Henry Goddard Leach on the Upper East Side of New York City. They have a long interview. Over the next few days they meet several more times, first at the Leaches' and then at Brenda's house in Stamford, Connecticut.

—*Roland Huntford,* Nansen: The Explorer as Hero, *published in Great Britain by Gerald Duckworth & Co. Ltd. in 1997, and by Abacus Books, London, 2001.*

April 25th, 1929

I

Dear Brenda,

You cannot possibly understand what your letter means to me, it is as if a flood of strength suffuses my whole body and soul, and I feel that you are near. How very sweet of you to write so soon. I needed it badly as I felt rather lonely. And what a letter! Just you as I was sure you must be. Free and upright, who scorns to pose as another than what you are. With the full confidence and real love, not wishing to hide anything, knowing that I will understand you and will understand everything, and will love you if possible still more. What an irresistible attraction towards you, what a warm feeling of tenderness, also because you wish me to know you exactly as you are. And I feel the same desire; there is not a corner of my heart or soul which I do not wish you to look into—not because I think that there may not be much which is ungraceful or offensive, but simply because it is all parts of my own self, and you have to know it. I have a feeling that I could talk to you about everything, as I have never had before, and you would always understand. It is strange how veracity gives a clearly wholesome feeling.

Your love-affairs puzzle me a little. You speak about the love affairs that you told me about; but I do not remember. You told me that you had had several lovers, and I thought it was quite natural, but I did not understand that you had had one for five years lately, because I understood you to say that you did not approve of lovers, and that was not because you could not have had them, which certainly I did not doubt. You say now that this 5 years affair is smashing with a kind of terrible speed—you cannot expect me to be sorry. But your lover has anger and hatred for you which you deserve, you say. I doubt that; why should you deserve it? Why should you be blameworthy? Is it because you love him no longer? How very strange that the disintegration of that long affair should begin just before you met me. Could it really

31

have anything to do with me and our relations? But you knew nothing about me! It is, however, equally strange that as I told you, when I got your first letter, I already felt an inexplicable attraction towards you, I longed to meet you, and had a vague anticipation that I would like you very much, and that perhaps you would like me too (how conceited I am!). And after I had heard your father speak about you, I was decided that I had to meet you, and I did not doubt that we would understand each other, and had much in common. I cannot say that there was anything special in that first letter, it was certainly nothing unusual that a lady asked for an interview, but there was something in the way in which you expressed yourself, or perhaps something more which I thought I read between the lines. And I had that letter with me, and your second one too, on my journey west, and I read it again and keenly regretted all the time more and more, that I had not made a special effort and gone out of my way to meet you, already during those first days I had in New York. In some respects that might have made a difference of some importance. But anyhow, what a great thing it was that we met at last. How distinctly I remember you the first time in that blue, tight coat that suited you so well, trimmed with fur. How very, very good-looking you were! And then you proposed to go at once and meet your father, while I wished to speak with you alone, and the proposal made me feel just a little disappointed, but that was soon forgotten when we talked, and I got an impression that perhaps after all it was not merely an interview for some article you wanted.

II

YOU SAID THAT you were homosexual. I very much doubt that you really are. It is well enough that there has been physical relations, but you say that probably there will never be again. That does not indicate that it sticks very deeply in your nature, and is it not rather something that has been acquired by circumstances? You can love a man passionately with your whole body and your whole beautiful soul. You could not if you were really homosexual. But you have unusually strong sexual feelings, and you certainly need satisfaction. If your man were there, you would have no craving for others. Is that not so? When I came home my very nice sister-in-law (78 years old) was very ill and thought she was dying. She has a friend, a lady, since 40 years, who during the last years has lived in the house with her, since my brother-in-law died. This lady has loved my sister-in-law from the very beginning with what was obviously a homosexual feeling, though I am certain there was never any physical relation of any kind. My sister-in-law loved her husband above everything in this world, and when he died life had lost its value for her. Nevertheless she tolerated this friend, and took her into the house. In the beginning, 40 years ago, I warned my sister-in-law against a friendship of this kind, it might easily develop into something that would not please her. During late years it has become more and more unbearable, and she has got such an aversion to her friend that the latter had to leave the house for some time, then she got so bad a conscience that she had to call her back. But now when she thought she was dying, she could not stand even to see her friend, and we had to keep her away. Now when my sister-in-law is probably recovering, I do not know what can be done, the friend ought to be sent away, but on the other hand I am afraid that that would break her heart. So the question is very complicated indeed.

This made me think of you, darling, though there may be very little resemblance; but I am so afraid of such relations, I believe they so very often cause the one part, for whom it is not natural, much pain and serious trouble, and I feel uneasy about you. My consolation is that you said she has also another friend. How dear and sweet you are, who writes so frankly about your relations and sexual impulses, and do not wish to glaze them over for the sake of your feelings toward me, and says you "will never be so with me though you have been too many times with others." Can I help loving you doubly for it, dear darling?

You have many good ideas about love, marriage, etc., and are sure you could easily convert me, you say. I am sure you have, but perhaps it would not be necessary to convert me very much.

How very sweet of you to be arrested with agony after we parted because you had not made me come home with you. Oh yes, it would have been wonderful, a last farewell! But it was obviously difficult, and we ought to be thankful for what we had, and I am more than I can say for everything you gave me. And I have the wonderful memories to live in, whenever I wish to have a happy moment. Yes, how perfectly wonderful it was, and how good and dear you were, and how beautiful, darling. Though I miss you every moment more than I can say, still how rich I am. You see, recollection is the only Paradise from which we cannot be turned out.

III

THAT IT IS IN YOUR POWER to do very very much for me, if you could be with me, is certain. You promise me you could make me ten times a greater man than I am; at least you could make me know what I am. Yes I think you are right, though I am not really much, chiefly a dreamer, with some scattered attempts at action, still I feel I would grow in your company; and if there is something perhaps of real value in me, it is what was never done; but you would see it, and might transform at least something of it into action. What a pity that we cannot work together! What a wonderful life that would be. You could give me so very, very much, but I know and feel keenly that I could give you a great deal too, and have the conceited confidence that you would not grow smaller by the contact. How really absurd it is, so short is life, and still we cannot arrange it and these few flying years as we know would be great and wonderful—if I did not know it before, your letter has made me feel it still more intensely. I never received any letter like it, never experienced such a revelation of a personality that I could adore and love, and give myself to without reserve.

Since I left you I have had to write some articles; but how I have missed you also then, I know how much you could have helped me, and how you could have given me advice. One article was a summary of the humanitarian work I have helped to carry out since

34

the war, for the *Current History Magazine*, it could perhaps have been quite good if you had been with me. The other was a preface to a new edition of Capt. Robert Scott's account of his first expedition, "The Voyage of the 'Discovery.'" I believe I could also have made something nice out of that with your help. His end was really tragic and great, at least in some respects. I wonder whether you know much about it and whether you have ever read his diary from his last expedition and his last death march? It is worth reading and is a remarkable human document. But now I have another task before me. I have promised to write, for my friend Henry [Goddard] Leach of *The Forum*, an article on my religion and views of existence and the future of humanity and the world, and then I shall miss you, your views, your judgment and your opinion more than ever. How easy if you were here, and how I would love to write it with you. But without you now?—I do not know how that will be, I shall feel very lonely and uncertain; and miss you for every line. You will know it, and will know how much you could give me. As it is, I fear that I shall not be able to put into words that much which I feel in my innermost self, and which I think might really be of some little value, as it may perhaps differ from what many others think, but it would agree with your views, I am sure. Well, I do not know yet what can come out of it, and whether it may be very shocking to many people? Anyhow I will not mind that; it will not shock you, I know.

I just received a letter from Mr. Adams the Secretary of your Navy, answering the several questions I had made about the possibility of help with the arrangement of our station in Alaska (Fairbanks) and the erection of a mooring mast there, etc. It is very discouraging, as the Navy cannot see its way to spend any money to help us. And now I do not know what to do, and have a keen regret that I left your country too soon. If your government is unable to assist us, at least with the loan of 8000 gas-cylinders which we need for the refilling of the air ship when we come to Alaska, I do not understand how we shall be able to find the means necessary to get these cylinders, as they will decidedly be too expensive if we shall be obliged to buy them. In that case it looks as if the expedition may become impossible to carry out. You will understand

35

that I feel very uncomfortable. For my own sake I do not mind so very much, I have so many other things which I wish to do if possible, but still it is most regrettable, when so much has been done, and so much time spent, then to give it up; it cannot be, and I have to do my utmost to find some way out of course. But again I miss you keenly, darling— Goodnight! I feel I am tired, I long for you. To rest and forget …

April 26th, 1929

IV

I SUPPOSE this long letter ought to come to an end and to be sent in order to reach you, though I hate to say goodbye, and could go on talking with you forever. How much I have got to say and to tell you, and how much to discuss, and I wish to hear your views of soul and body. You wish me to love you "for a long time, at least until we meet again, for then it will be easy to entrance me again." Surely, you do not even need my presence for that—your letter can obviously do it. You feel that you "can pour out, suffuse me with a warmth, a radiance, a fulfillment such as no one in the world has or will ever experience." Oh, darling, I feel that I am already suffused with part of that warmth, you are near me here in my tower, I see you there, radiant in the sunshine, pouring in through the window, behind you some sketches of the Northern Lights, how appropriate! Oh that beautiful body! The house of a wonderful soul! The graceful movements of the limbs, the play of the muscles, the tremulous quivering of the flesh, "the act-poems of eyes, hands, hips, and bosoms," as Walt Whitman calls it.

> *"O I say these are not the parts and poems*
> *of the body only, but of the soul.*
> *O I say now these are the soul."*

I love you, darling, "with all my wisdom and all my folly."
Fridtjof

How very nice that you like that name. I am sending you the two volumes about my Fram expedition [*Fram over Polhavet, Farthest North* (1897)]. Please do not read more than something here and there. It is much too long; but perhaps you may find something which will interest you, and perhaps some glimpses of the incurable dreamer. I will send you more books later. I love your name, Brenda, it is the fire of your soul, and your radiant burning eyes.

Is this address you give in your last letter better than the printed one on your envelopes?

Sunday, April 28th, 1929

Dear Brenda, yesterday morning I sent you a long letter, and yesterday evening a new letter from you! (of April 10th after receipt of my letter with the pilot of April 6th. Why did you not get it before 9th?) What delight! Though it makes me wild with longing, still it makes me indescribably happy to read what you have written. You pour out your dear beautiful soul. Yes, it was, it is sad that I did not come home with you that last time, you would have given me so much more of yourself to remember, and enjoy and be happy about, and I could have given you so much to remember, I believe; which I had not given you. But as I said in my last letter, I believe we have so much to be grateful for, as it is, at least I have, and I feel so wonderfully happy and strong, although I do not have you. You were so sweet, so dear, as I never had dreamt [anyone] could ever be. I cannot possibly describe it—such touching, perfect confidence. I live again every moment of it—when you came in and dropped everything so naturally without reserve, my darling, it was heaven. And when I came in to you, and you awoke, and that smile! it was too heavenly; and how keenly I felt that you loved me—But I was very tired that day, mentally and physically worn out, had had too much to go through and to think of.

Yes, how distinctly I remember when I came into the Leaches' drawing (room), and saw you, I still see you in this moment as if you were standing here before me, as beautiful and charming, and I walked up and took your hands. Could I help it? It seemed so quite natural, only it would have been still more natural to embrace you. But I did

37

not understand that you were alarmed, or even horrified, I ought to probably, but I felt so confident, and did not think of anything more than that I was so quite unusually happy to be with you, and had no thoughts of what might happen. And when you proposed, or at least said, that I could come home with you, well, I cannot explain what I felt then! And when I had been in the telephone and came up again I took you in my arms, and really you did not resist, at least not much. But when we were going down the stairs you began to say something which sounded like a reservation, and I got a little fright, but fortunately you could not finish just then, and afterward I did not dare to ask what it was, nor did I wish to know; and fortunately, you did not come back to it. But then once later you said that you did not approve of lovers, or were afraid of them, perhaps it was. That frightened me again, as certainly I least of all wished to do any harm, or cause you any trouble; but happily I heard nothing more about it, you were only as wonderfully sweet and good; and it is my hope that you do not regret it, and never will, and that it does not <u>really</u> give you any compunction of any kind?

How I wish I could be with you. I feel anxiety about you; I believe you need me, and I am convinced that I could be much more for you and give you more ecstasy, force, and tranquility than anybody else. There you have my megalomania. But when I cannot be there, what then? That there is no one in the world who can give as much as you can, and never was, is certain; and it makes me more happy than I possibly can say to feel that you can and will, and that you know it.

Brenda, my darling, all you say about your love and your feelings make me so deliriously happy, and that you feel that we must meet again. It cannot be otherwise; let us trust to time, fancy to meet in some undisturbed place—and marry, so wonderful a dream, I dare not dream it. How I wish to have a child with you; I am convinced it would be something quite unusual. Why cannot life be like our dreams. Is it cowardice, or rather fear of doing too much harm to others?

My darling, I must not prevent you from working, and therefore

38

I ought not to write any more. I am so glad that you can work and become rich and independent, I only wish to see your work or at least some part of it! Do let me. But do not speak about the gas-bottles, that would be a poor way of spending the money. I must work too, I am just in the middle of my article about my creed, etc ["What I Believe," for Henry Leach's *Forum*, Dec. 1929]. How I miss you, and how much I wish to discuss every question with you, about the purpose of existence and about immortality, about the nature of the soul, its origins etc etc. How many splendid suggestions you could give me. I am what people would call a hopeless materialist you see, though really I am not materialistic at all! And I love you, Brenda, my darling, more than anybody else can do, though I am sure the love does not last beyond the limits of this one life!

I am writing about the soul and the body, and the usual consolation people find in the belief in the immortality of the soul. It seems to me so strange that intelligent people who really think can actually be convinced of such an absurdity as it seems to me. Fancy the soul which is so entirely dependent on the body, which is simply a manifestation of its processes, should live on and the body not. Fancy this soul, which can be entirely changed, bit by bit, by changes of the body. One can cut all your specific qualities away slice by slice from your brain till nothing but a low animal is left. Which soul is it that is going to live? The last one, the original? And not only the brain, other parts of the body as well. A little change in the function of your thyroid gland may entirely change your disposition and character. And what about the sexual glands? Removal or only some change or slight encroachment on the functions of an apparently quite insignificant part of them, what a perfect change it can produce in the whole nature of a man (and I suppose a woman too?), in his soul, his character, his whole personality. Fancy the eunuch or on the other hand the sexual criminal and the sexual lunatic. Which soul is it that is immortal? The one before or the one after the radical changes? And I am quite unable to understand the consolation or the satisfaction in believing that my soul is going to live on after the body, which gave it all its characteristic qualities, its personality? What an empty, colorless existence. O no, we men are too greedy, we are not satisfied with this one life, and not with the idea that something is going to live after us in the effects of our acts, our thoughts, and in our descendants.

Anyhow I love you, my darling, with my whole body and soul, and I love your body and soul, and cannot distinguish between them. But I doubt that I could love you in another world, as I would not know what to love. But therefore when one really loves, there is inevitably a craving to melt together, body and soul, and there is a longing that the poem should be continued in a new individual, a fusion, a melding together of the two, a lasting, growing, healthy product of their love. So much there is to say about all this, but I cannot now.

How well I understand that you love your brother. He is a fine specimen of the human race. But so are all of you, as I told you before, a quite remarkable family.

In the end of the week I will go into the woods shooting capercaillie (cock of the woods). I love that, it is so nice in the awakening spring, and we shoot them in the early morning, first at daybreak, at the first indication of dawn, when the cock is sitting in the pine tree calling, or also walking to and fro on the ground, waiting for the hen. You may think it is cruel to disturb him in his passing, but perhaps it is a happy moment to die in. I wish you were there, how you would enjoy that life in the woods, the campfire in the night, and the whole mystery of the awakening nature. There is the life, where I feel most at home; I believe I am a son of the great woods. After some days there in the woods I have to go to Berlin for a meeting of our International Society to discuss our preparations for the Polar expedition on May 12th and 13th, and then I have a meeting I have called in Geneva on May 16th of representatives of various governments, to discuss the legal positions etc. of the Refugees, particularly the Russian Refugees. I shall probably be back here about May 20th, and then perhaps I will find a letter from you. I do not wish to disturb you in your work, my darling, but still please, do write, at least a few lines. You cannot imagine what it is to receive your letters. Perhaps it would be best if you do not use envelopes with your name and address outside, and also if you sometimes could write my address on the envelope with typewriter, it might perhaps cause less attention, when there is some variation. And see to it that the envelope is closed safely with the gum. Much harm can be done by an open or opened letter. I miss more than I can say a picture of you, have you got one, or several, to send me?

I wish I could see you sun burnt, as you speak about; I am sure it makes you still more beautiful, but not on account of the eyes. I cannot agree with you in what you say about the dark eyes, that they look so opaque. At least, yours certainly do not. So radiant, so wonderful, I could see straight through them, into your dear lovely soul; I can see them still!

But dear me! I said long ago that I had to finish, and here I am still writing. I enclose a picture, I just found, which I took a few years ago. I thought I might send it, but burn it, if you think so. How I would have loved to take one of you, my darling, the free, independent child of Nature, still with such wonderfully fine culture.

April 29th, 1929

I have just got telegrams from Washington & New York. It looks better now. They hope to get the gas bottles from the Army (the War department), and we may possibly manage to overcome the difficulties. I also am informed that Wilkins [George Hubert Wilkins, Australian Polar explorer 1888-1959] has definitely given up his expedition under the ice in a submarine, upon which I heartily congratulate him. It is certainly true that many good and ingenious projects have been declared by the wise authorities to be absurd, but it is not therefore certain that all projects which are declared to be absurd are good and ingenious. Now I understand that Wilkins is going to join an expedition as correspondent for the American press, and he is going with the "Graf Zeppelin" on its next trip to America. My darling, why couldn't you be the correspondent for the press? What a splendid correspondent you would make, and what wonderful accounts you could write! And I could certainly help you.

They should be marvellous! Fancy if such a thing could happen, or at least you could come to Alaska, to Fairbanks! There could be much to write about there.

But now I really must not keep you any longer from your work, and I have to work too, there is much waiting. But it is hard to tear myself away, for I love you so.

> Still goodbye,
> ever yours,
> Fridtjof

May 1st, 1929

Dear Brenda,

I had just brought my letter to you to the post office yesterday when I received your letter of the 13th; and again a torrent of warmth, and happiness and love rushed through my whole body and soul. I cannot tell you what it feels like to see your letter, to open it, and then to read it, o heaven! It is always you, as different from all others; in whatever you say, you have your dear way of saying it—how I love you, my darling. But you must not regret the letters you sent me, and say that they were too ardent. Can they ever be? It makes me almost sad; what then about the letters I have sent you? Shall I have to regret them? Shall I be more sensible? How can one help it? I do not wish to hide my thoughts and feelings, and I hope you do not wish to either. I am sure we both wish to be quite natural and quite frank with each other, that need not make us supine and weak, as you are so afraid of. On the contrary I feel it gives me new strength and force, and ideas, it increases my vitality. And even if I had been there, would it not have had this same effect, at least after some days? I am sure it would with me—new life, new vigor, new initiative, new craving to do something. In the beginning perhaps, there might have been more ecstasy and wonderful happiness, which made one forget one's own personality and sink everything into that of the other, as you are so afraid of. But don't you think that there would have been a marvelous strengthening 'regeneration' with it? Yes I long and wish to dive deep,

deep into, to be drowned in your personality, and I know I will absorb new strength by it, become a new and stronger, and better man by it, with a new will, a new ambition to live, and to act, I will again think the deeds worth doing; and all this without sapping you, but, as I do hope, giving you, too, new strength and vitality (if that is possible?).

I wish I could see you punishing yourself by the "most violent exercise." It reminds me of the ascetics of medieval times. I did not expect you to be very ascetic, but I understand that is a way you are, and very much so really, with a will of steel. I wish I could see your acrobatics and could run with you, though I know you would beat me.

I am very, very glad and proud to think that you like my Armenian book [*Armenia and the Near East* (1928)], though really I was in despair when I wrote it, as I thought it was so very dull, and contained so little, and I felt there was something more and better to be said, but could not find words for it. I am sorry to have to disillusion you, the English in that book is not mine, it has been translated from the Norwegian original and I have only revised it, and so it is with most of my popular books, "Adventure" [*Adventure: and Other Papers*, Leonard & Virginia Wolff (1927)] was however written by me in English, as were all my scientific works.

I like to hear you speak about your work, and wish I could be there and stimulate you without disturbing you. We would both of us work. How would that be? Send me your articles, I long to read them.

How very nice that you shall write on architecture and that you wish to see my son [Odd Nansen, 1901-1973, architect, author, humanitarian]. By all means do, he is a very nice boy, and you will like him, but please do not fall in love with him. He is very much nicer than I am, and is really quite good looking. I wish you will see him. If you write or phone, say that I am very anxious that you should see him, and, if you think so, that I have written to you about it. You might be interested in some of his drawings, and his plans for new cities. I believe there is an exhibition going on just now in the Grand Central Station, where some of his drawings are also exhibited. He is really quite gifted I think, and has ideas of his own about architecture, and

43

he begins to feel that something quite new in architecture may come out of the new American construction and methods of building, and that concrete is bound to result in a new style of the future. His wife [Kari] is Norwegian and very nice. I hope you will like them.

And now, goodbye dear Brenda, my darling. I hope you will have peace to work, and will not think that I am disturbing you too much with my letters. I long to hear from you again, always. I love you, and I always long for you.

Fridtjof

In the Woods
May 7th, 1929

Dear Brenda,

I long for you, and you are always in my thoughts, and I long for a new letter from you. It is really strange: I opened some paper or periodical and there on the one page I saw in big letters the name Ole Gabriel Ueland, and an article about your grandfather. On the opposite page there was an article headed Brendenesle (i.e. burning nettle). The first part of the word was your dear name of course, the second part reminded me of the Scotch peasant song:

> *"Touch not the nettle, lest haply it sting ye,*
> *Only see green as the bracken grows,*
> *Love not the love that never can win ye*
> *For the bands of love are ill to loose."*

Nevertheless I am not afraid of touching the nettle, and I love, love, love, and do not wish to loose the bands, nor can I, my dear darling. I wonder how you feel now, and what your mood is, whether you still take the violent exercise? How very, very dear you are. The shooting has been poor hitherto, full winter with knee-deep snow, something quite unheard of in May. But now we have had pouring rain, and the snow greatly gone. Today we are going further into the wood and hope it will be better, but I am not going away from you. A thousand greetings, goodbye.

I love you my darling ever yours,
Fridtjof

In the Woods
May 9th, 1929

Dear Brenda,

Here I am again writing to you instead of working, but I have to. You are always in my thoughts, my dear darling, and I must talk with you. I wish you were here, you and I alone. I long to live this life with you, far away from all the trivialities of the rushing world; have you as you are, as you sprung, noble and glorious, from the hand of Nature, in all your dear beauty, so delightfully naked and free from all conventionalities, your deep genuine feelings, your passions, your intellect—o, why are you not here, we belong to each other. It is as if I am no more myself without you, my darling.

I wander through the woods in the night, I hear the mysterious sounds of the solitude, I hear the red robin awakening just as there is a faint glow of the day in the east, his first tremulous sounds. I hear the capercaillie (large grouse) beginning to call in his dark pine, his first faint love-calling. I hear the hens answering in their passionate longing for love and propagation. I see the day gradually growing. I hear the capercaillies fighting, fighting for the hens. I hear the victorious ones embracing their hens in wild passion, beating their wings so it sounds through the wood, while the beaten cocks fly away. —And then the sun rises, the glorious king of light and activity, and the wonders of the night have vanished like a dream.

Always this mysterious "call of the wild," back to nature, back to our origin, to the innermost in us, a bath of renewal in the primitive feelings in us, the genuine self. The big woods, the great, free solitude, far away from the banal, empty decorations of artificial life.

But behind and above it all, my thoughts seek you Brenda, my darling, and I cannot long for anything without you.

"Among the woods my birth was
Amid hills and waters blue,
But flat and bare the earth was
That since has not my view.
Though wheat-land and rye-land
On fertile plains be good
My soul longs for my land
For hill and wave and wood."
—WILLIAM WORDSWORTH

Yes I feel like that, and still I cannot feel at home anywhere without you.

But no, I must not write to you any longer, I must return to my work, though it is so hard to say goodbye. And how much there is in connection with that work, which I want to discuss with you, about morality, love, altruism, and so many, many other questions. I long to hear your free, independent views. I wonder whether they can be still more radical than mine? Well some day we will compare them.

May 12th, 1929

I am in the train through Sweden to Berlin, [about to face] all kinds of difficulties and annoying questions. I hate it. And then, after that, Geneva with another meeting and other worries. I shall be glad to be on my way back again. I am so sorry that there was not time to send you some of my other books. I will do it when I come back, but some of them I may possibly have to get from England. And then I will also send you some pictures, though they are not much to look at, still I wish you to have them. Dear me, how shaky that train is!

I wonder how you are, and what you are doing! How much you think of me? It seems a long time since I heard from you, and there will be few letters in Berlin, perhaps in Geneva. I love you, Brenda; can you ever understand how much?

I am crossing the sea from Sweden to Germany. Glorious sunshine. I miss you more than ever. Why are you not here? I can still

remember a strange dream I had last night in the train. There was a very lovely woman, who liked me, and came to me, just as I was going out alone, and she asked why I wanted to go alone, and would leave her behind with the others, she said she wanted to be with me. But how strange, she had not your face, I do not know who she was, I do not know that face, but it was very lovely, and I liked her. I can still see her, I was standing on the steps of the staircase looking up at her, a little above me. Probably it was you, only you had changed somewhat, but it was your body in a gray dress. How funny and stupid dreams can be, and still they may put us in a mood for a long while after, even though we do not think of it. Goodbye my darling, I am afraid you will soon hear from me again. Do I write too much? I shall try to be more sensible, and think of my work instead of you; but that is hardly possible, for you are always with me in my work. The article about my "creed" is making slow progress, but dear one, how I miss you! Yours,
Fridtjof

I am a universe of wandering feelings, impressions come and go like:

> *"The voices of the wandering wind,*
> *That moan for rest, and rest*
> *Can never find."*
> [FROM, "THE DEVA'S SONG," BY EDWIN ARNOLD]

There is no rest except in
Your arms, my darling.

Geneva
May 16th, 1929

Dear Brenda,
Here I find a piece of paper, how can I use it better than for writing a few lines to you, my darling. I had hoped to find a letter from you when I arrived last midnight. There were many letters sent from Norway, but none from you; it seems such a long time since your last letter,

and I am longing so for word from you. Am I very unreasonable? – I was in Berlin a day having meetings, and discussing our preparations for the polar expedition. Then I left in the evening and was in Friedrichshafen and saw Dr. Eckener the next day. I discussed our places with him, and what he has got to say about our preparations and our gas-cylinders etc. when he now comes to America. I went over the ship, it is really a fine construction, and more than room enough for all we need, men + dogs + equipment. They should have started yesterday morning, but had to postpone it on account of much wind in the Atlantic and on the coast of France. So I had to leave again without seeing them off, and came here last night. I wonder whether the ship started this morning? And whether you will see it when it comes to New York?

Today I have had meetings discussing the Russian and Armenian Refugee problems all day, and am more than tired of it. And now I have to dress and go out to dinner, and continue the discussion, and you will not be there, and I have to close this and tell you what you do not know and have never heard before that I love you!

Night

I am back from a very dull party, and just want to say goodnight. O why are you not here, why are you not in that bed waiting for me? Framing your wonderful head on that pillow, your radiant eyes open, your smile, your lovely arms stretched out towards me, your beautiful body, o, what heavenly happiness! But some day, yes some day. I love you more than words can express Brenda, my darling.

  Yours,
  Fridtjof

Hotel Adlon Berlin
May 20th, 1929

Dear Brenda,
I am in Berlin, tomorrow back in Norway. It is Whitsuntide. It is spring, it is sunshine, flowers, green beaches, glittering waters, and

there is a lady, very pretty, charming, we are good friends, and life ought to be smiling, but – it makes me feel still more lonely – why am I not with you, my darling? Where are you, with whom are you, what are you doing? I long for you more than ever because I love you. I am leaving with the train tonight. Will there be a letter for me when I get home? I hope it will be, I need it badly now. But I feel happy nevertheless, I know that you think of me, that you love me.

Do you think I am silly to write such stupid letters? I wonder. I am continually in such a strange mood, and cannot sit down quietly and collect my thoughts. I miss you too much perhaps, in every way. I want to be near you, to speak to you, there is so much I wanted to tell you; but I cannot write it down on paper, then it seems banal and not very important. But why should it be so important? Perhaps life is not so very important after all, though it is the only one we have. Still you and I are important nevertheless, in that we belong to each other.

In the train through Sweden
May 21st, 1929

On my way back to wife and daughter, but not to you! Will there be a letter waiting? What have I accomplished on this journey? Very little. The accident with the Zeppelin in France is not good for our expedition, though it is not the ship but the motors which have failed. Nevertheless it makes a bad impression, I suppose, and does not improve our prospects in your country.* And the refugee work? Well, I have to continue with it, though without any wish or interest, simply a dull feeling of duty because I cannot be replaced. But it seems all of it so very indifferent, both that, and expedition, and the rest. What do I really wish to do? Life seems so meaningless; we are marionettes moved by something else, and still they want to go on forever. Why do I write when I am in such a depressed mood? It cannot be very cheering for you. But I miss you so badly, I wish to lay my head in your lap, and just to feel your hands and your body, and hear your voice, and look into your dear eyes. – But do not believe that my love and my longing kill my energy and my enterprise. No, it is only the doubt whether the doings are worth the while. It is the feeling that there are things so much more valuable to be done, and that one will never get as far before the last act is finished. Yes, this feeling that precious time is passing, wasted!

But no now more than enough about myself, it is not interesting, and soon I will be in another mood and can perhaps write something more sensible. I do hope that you are getting on alright with your work. I long to see something of it. How nice it would be if I could be there and we could help each other. Don't you think we could? I am sure of it. You could help me a great deal of course, and perhaps I could help, or at least stimulate you a little too. Fancy how nice we could have it together, and how happy we would be in a world of our own.

> Goodbye, my darling
> Fridtjof

❦ The Graf Zeppelin was a large, German-made, hydrogen-filled, passenger-carrying dirigible. During its operating life, from 1928 to 1937, the airship made 590 flights, covering more than a million miles.... The airship was almost lost just over half a year after its maiden flight while attempting to make its second trip to the United States in May 1929. On May 16, the airship lost power in two of its five engines forcing its captain, Dr. Hugo Eckener, to abandon the trip and return to Friedrichshafen, Germany. While flying against a stiff headwind the next afternoon, two of the remaining three engines also failed. The airship crash-landed about ten miles from Toulon, France.

On August 1st, 1929, the Graf Zeppelin made another attempt to cross the Atlantic arriving in Lakehurst, New Jersey on August 4th, 1929. Four days later, the airship departed Lakehurst on another daring enterprise—a complete circumnavigation of the globe. —EU

> Lysaker
> May 22nd, 1929

Darling Brenda,

What happiness! Your dear letter of Apr. 27th was there when I came [home] last night. New life, new vigor, new vitality. What wonderful witchcraft do you possess? I felt your lovely arms around my neck, your lips, your breasts, your lap, your thighs, your whole, beautiful body, and the heavenly fire through my limbs and my brain—and the spring is there, more beautiful in Norway than anywhere on Earth. Here from my window in my tower, I see the maidenly birches in their bridal veils against the dark pine wood; —there is nothing like the birch in the spring. I do not exactly know why, but it is like you, to me you have the same maidenliness—and the sun is laughing, and the fjord out there is glittering, and existence is beauty!

This morning I got your letter of May 8th, in which you say that you are afraid you have written me too perfervid letters. You frighten me. What shall I say about my letters? But, my darling, can our letters ever be too hot if we feel it so? Can we not be quite frank with each other, and say exactly what we feel, without thinking too much of whether it is nice or not? At least I know that you cannot say too much, but the more the better; it does me more good than you can imagine, gives me new vigour, new inspirations, new hope. And perhaps it gives you something too? And more than if we are so very circumspect and sensible. And if we think it right we can burn the letters afterward, when they have brought their message and fulfilled their destination. But if it disturbs you, darling, and you therefore think it is better not, of course I will try to be very sensible; though you ask me not to tear anything up, but send you everything I write to you; and I can write what I please. You amuse me. Well, I will do so, and will not think of being so very sensible, until you tell me that I have to. Then I also hope that you will not be so very circumspect either, or rather that you will not think of it, but be perfectly frank, and say things as they are. After all isn't that the most natural, and perhaps also the most wholesome?

Did I really ask you to destroy my letter? I have forgotten; but I dare say that it was pretty hot, and my thought was probably that such things are only fit to be read for the moment, while the right conditions are there; but not to be read later with cold blood. It is, I hope, needless to say that I could not possibly have the slightest anxiety about your discretion, such a thought could not enter my brain, my dearest darling. Perhaps it is wise to destroy the letters, I can destroy yours too if you think so, so that they shall never come into the wrong hands; though I must confess that it will to me be like murder to burn your dear letters, your children, a part of your soul.

Yes, you are right, love is indeed very strange. That wonderful mixture of adoration, the most tender feelings, the highest, sublimest mental ecstasy, the love of your soul and all that it is, and then your body and the wildest sexual passion—soul and body in one, you cannot and do not wish to separate the one from the other. I long to be with you all the day, first to take in your thoughts, to give you all mine, my whole soul, I do not wish to accomplish anything without your help, without you having a part in it, without knowing that you approve of it. Not that I wish you to agree in everything—no, two independent souls free born, and still I wish them to mingle. But then, I also long to be with you every night, sleep in your arms, feel the whole of your body, press your beautiful lips, feel your hips, your lovely thighs, sink deep into you, melt into one with you, feel you passionately trembling in utter abandonment, you and I lost, everything else disappeared— time and space gone, we sink into eternity—o dear, it is something more than merely physical.

II

IT IS STRANGE indeed what you say, that until you knew me, you believed yourself to be almost sexless! How very wonderful! A more vigorous, violent sexual passion, a more perfect sensual rapture I cannot imagine, but it seemed such a natural part of your intense, strong personality and of your splendid, healthy body, just a perfect type of the race. I long wildly to be with you again, and what happiness to hear you say that you would walk through machine gun fire to spend a night with me. I only wish I could. I am afraid I would do it gladly. It may be madness, I am not sure though, for after all it is perhaps the climax, the apotheosis of life—the old tale of Sigurd riding through the fire to sleep with Brynhild [A Norse tale of gallantry, deception, longing and unrequited love.] But surely, we would have no sword between us!

52

So far last night when I was interrupted by my daughter [Liv] and son-in-law [Andreas L. Høyer] coming to supper. Now I must try to finish and mail this, as I have to work. I will not tear it up, though maybe, it is very hot, but I wouldn't even if it had been still hotter, because it is me, I cannot help it, and it belongs to you, my darling, and I trust it will not disturb you too much?

What you say about your love affair with your woman friend interests me of course very much. Now I understand that I made a mistake when you spoke about your "lover" before, and I thought it was a man. It was your "mistress." But of course, it is extremely difficult for me to understand the various sides and emotions of such a relation. I wonder whether it did not, to some extent at least, come about because you were disappointed, disgusted with your love affairs and adventures with men. But nevertheless your strong sexual passion, without your knowing it perhaps, needed satisfaction. This is obviously connected with some of the deepest mysteries in our nature, inextricably connected with the sex, the propagation of the race, etc.— You say that your feeling, passion, for her has been all along so epicene and mild; but isn't there in such a relation some difference between the two partners, both physically and mentally? Does not the one partner represent more the male side and the other the female side? The one more active, aggressive, the other more passive, receptive? I wonder whether the passion can ever be very strong, or wild, and whether in spite of everything, it is not rather a substitute?

Well, these are of course very complicated [matters], but also very interesting psychological and perhaps also physiological questions, which it is very difficult for an "outsider" to have any definite opinion about.

It is strange that you should just study the life of Napoleon, with whom I thought you had such a remarkable likeness the first time I saw you. Of course he was a remarkable man. Compared with other rulers, he had naturally the great advantage of being quite unusually

53

gifted. Whether one may call him a genius is another question. Anyhow, he was a unique specimen of man and of the male sex, and thus highly interesting, although one cannot or will not admire his character, there perhaps were his shortcomings. I do not think, however, that Taine's, [*The Modern Regime*, by Hippolyte Adolfe Taine], judgment of him can be justified. It is extremely one sided, and certainly Napoleon was not [such] a small man as he makes him [out to be]. But of course every man may have his weak points or his weak moments and when you know them, you may think that no man is great. No man is great for his servant, they say, but perhaps that is not fair. It may also be because the servant has not got the ability to appreciate his great sides, and only sees the small ones. It would interest me keenly to hear your opinions about all these questions. O, dear me, how much we have to talk about when we meet. I look much forward to get your article, whether it is "cheese" or not I do not mind. It is enough that you have written it, and that it tells me at least something about what you are doing and thinking, and you may safely leave it to me to have my opinion about its value. I will soon send you some more books of mine, I hope "Farthest North" reached you safely.

How nice that Julie [Ueland, wife of Brenda's brother Sigurd] has been with you, I am sure she is good company. I wonder whether you spoke about me, and whether she found out that you like me?

III

THERE ARE SO MANY THINGS I wanted to write about, I could go on for ever, but I must stop I suppose, and try to do some work. I hope to hear from you soon again, you cannot understand what it is to get your letters. Do write, even if it is not so very much, and do not be afraid of not being sufficiently circumspect and sensible please. Be not afraid of the heat, it is wholesome you know, and just write what you feel and think. You know that I love you, with all my heart and all that is me.

Fridtjof

54

I do not know how many letters I have sent you on my last journey to Berlin and Geneva. I believe three at least, and the last one I mailed in Gōteborg [Gothenburg]. I hope you have got them, when you get this.

May 23rd, evening

O Brenda,

My darling, my girl, my mistress, my everything! I had written the letter and was going to mail it when yours of May 10th arrived this evening, and I must open the envelope again and add these few lines. Will write more soon. Oh, happiness, it is as if I had you here in my arms, and felt your lovely body pressed close to mine. You are a sorceress, indeed, you have tied me hand and foot, soul and body, everything, I am lost. I remember well before I had seen you, I was curious to know what you would be like, and whether perhaps there might be waiting some nice acquaintance. When after dinner with your sister I spoke to you about meeting, and touched your hand and you pressed mine just so much that I thought I could feel it, and you proposed that I might come to Stamford, I thought that perhaps it might develop into some more or less innocent adventure. But the adventure has, indeed, become a very serious one. You have perfectly entranced me, I am carried off my feet, and cannot reach ground any longer. When I try to recall how it all happened, I cannot quite remember, but I do remember how wonderfully sweet you were, how willingly you kissed me, how sweetly you gave yourself without resistance, though you had said that you were not certain that you approved of lovers. Oh my darling, what incredible happiness it is, and how madly I love you.

F.

May 31st, 1929

My dear, dear Brenda,

O joy! I have got a new glorious long letter from you of May 16th, and a flood of happiness and delight drowns my whole body and soul. I cannot possibly explain to you what it feels like, I wish I could. It is such a strange mixture of inspiration, exaltation, demand to do great things with sensual rapture, ecstasy, a delicious, voluptuous longing to be in your arms, to feel your whole wonderful body, to kiss you madly, to sink into you, to be surrounded by your wildest love, to be drowned and melted into one with you. O, my darling, you need not be afraid, it is very, very far from being sensible, and, certainly, I do not wish to be. I look at those two lovely pictures you have sent with your letter. I press them to my lips, and dream that it is yourself. That dear head, with the beautiful, strong, determined profile I love so much, and which struck me already the first time I saw you, and that splendid, athletic, supple body; I wish it were quite naked. I put my arms round that curved back, I lift you and press you against my body, I feel your arms round me, your burning kiss, your breasts, our bellies pressed and glued together, those strong, beautiful thighs clasping mine, I press delightfully in between them, flesh passionately trembling enclosed by quivering flesh, earth and heaven sunk into nothing—the juice of love—and wonder of a child is begotten.

O, my darling, do you think I am perfectly mad? But I feel like that, and you know it too. Should I not say it? It is yours though, however, I shall try to be a little more sensible.

There are so many things in your two last letters of May 10th (which I just received when I sent my last letter, was it the 25th?) and May 16th, I wanted to answer, if I only could take the time; but I have much work waiting, so probably I cannot write very much today. You are afraid that what you call your "wild letters" (though they are not very wild, unfortunately) may make an "uneasy stir in a tranquil life," but please don't think like that. You ought to know that it is just the other way, that you give me wonderful inspiration, and exaltation, a remarkable buoyancy, and your "wildness" is just like a refreshing bath in the fountain of life. So therefore, please let us be quite natural, and not afraid of what we feel and think, it is healthier I believe; and really I have no desire to hide anything from you, my darling.

It is interesting to read what you tell about our first meetings. Did I really, that first evening in your house, tell you about my poor adventures, and about the swim for the kayaks, with an arm across your shoulders and a hand on your thigh? Had I really time for that when there were so many much more important things to speak about? Was it in order to make some impression on you, I wonder? Or perhaps rather, did I talk along, glad to have something of the past to talk about, in order to hide my real feelings. But o, what a wonderful evening, with the mysterious night before us, what an exaltation, a wonderful elevating feeling of happiness. It was as if my whole interior opened and absorbed your whole beautiful being, and I felt that really we belonged to each other, that you possessed me, and I had no desire to be free again.

How wonderful it is to hear you say that you know that you can complete me, and that you are not complete without me. I do feel that it is so, and cannot be otherwise. But what [good] luck that your strange love affair has kept you from marrying again!

How very strange, however, what you say that you have been "so cold, tranquil, and collected," and do not "suppose you have a romantic or a sentimental or a sexual thought once in a year in spite of the so-called love affair".… As I think I told you before my impression of you is quite different—a violent strong, healthy sexual passion which imperatively demanded satisfaction, and very much! A wonderful revelation, something quite unusual, so entirely carried away, lost, forgetting everything. O yes, so wonderful. Can that be only because "you belong to one," "are my girl," as you say? And "without me, sex means nothing to you," you say. How is that possible, how rich I am, what happiness!! Indeed you are "a sorceress, whom I cannot escape from."

But in your last letter (of May 16th) you say something that makes me a little uneasy. You say, "In my last letter I think I said how you were not to be 'true' to me as the saying goes etc." You have, however, said nothing of the kind in any letter I have received from you. Does it mean that there is one letter between that of May 10th (which I have now answered) and that of the 16th which I have not received?? I cannot bear the thought that a letter of yours should be lost, and that I should not get it. What an irreparable loss!! I hope that it cannot be so, and that you may only have thought of writing this without having done it. In your last letter you tell about your visit to the library on Monday the 13th and that the day before the first volume of "Farthest North" had just arrived (I hope you have got the second volume too, they were not sent simultaneously). You have, however, written nothing about this, but it is hardly probable that you should have written any letter between the 10th and the 16th I suppose? Because if so you would not probably tell about what happened on the 12th and the 13th? It would be well if you could tell me in the future the date of your previous letter, in order that I may know that I have got them all. I will try to do the same.

I will mail this now, and answer your last letter as soon as possible. I long to hear from you again Brenda my darling, for I love you more than you can understand.

Fridtjof

Friday, May 31st, 1929

I

BRENDA, MY DARLING, here I am again, but do not be afraid, I am very sensible. I mailed my letter to you in the middle of the day to catch the mail-train, and now I want to answer some points in your last letter. You are touching, indeed, when you say that I am not to be "true" to you. I understand you perfectly, my darling, and I think we agree entirely. I know well enough that you want me for yourself, and yourself alone; it would be unnatural if you did not. But in general I think the old ideas of possessing and consequent jealousy are more or less ruinous to real love. I do not understand why, when I really love a person, it gives me any right of possession, or why I should be jealous because I have a suspicion that the person also cares for somebody else? It seems also doubtful whether I have any right to demand that a woman must under no circumstance have any sexual intercourse with anybody else, if she loves me so much that she has "given herself" to me. Isn't it after all a very selfish and base idea? I wonder whether

58

most ideas as to sexual morality are not very old fashioned and not very moral on this as on other points?

It is of course another question whether one may love a person so much and so ardently that one cannot think of anybody else. But I suppose in many cases one may love a person sufficiently to wish to have sexual intercourse, but not so much that one could promise to belong to that one person alone forever or for any length of time. Would it in that case be more moral to abstain than not? I do not quite see why, unless it did harm to the other person or to oneself. But if it gives pleasure, satisfaction and more happiness to the other person, who may otherwise have to live in an unwholesome celibacy, I think it is morally right of course, even though it may not prevent sexual relations to somebody else as well. Celibacy is hardly good nor specially moral for any strong, healthy person, at least not for a normal man, but I believe also for a woman. You say that you were cold, tranquil, and collected but would it have been the same if you had lived in a real celibacy, even though your relationship did not perhaps give you any perfect satisfaction? Persons may of course be very different in this respect. Some people, and especially some women, I believe, may have very little sexual passion so that they are almost sexless and sexual intercourse gives them but little pleasure. They can easily live in celibacy, while for normal persons it is certainly otherwise, and you know what I think of you in this respect.

II

THERE IS ANOTHER SIDE of monogamy which I think we talked about. If you live with the same person always, and never learn to know others, you lose your opportunities of extending your experiences, of exploring human nature, of developing and completing yourself. And of course you never can learn to know another person as well as by sexual intercourse or should we rather call it erotic intercourse.

But no, this theoretical discussion has brought me far away from the concrete question: you and I. Of course that is different, we have had our experiences, both of us, and we love each other so fully, so blindly, that we cannot possibly long for or think of anybody else; and I do not really know what I would feel, if I thought you could. But I know that I love you so much, that it would not change my feeling as long as I was convinced that your real love was for me. I would try to understand.

♦ Nansen married his second wife, Sigrun, on December 17, 1919. Aware of his affairs, Sigrun nonetheless remained Nansen's wife until his death.

And now as to myself. Of course, I have had several friends and relations; but they all dwindled to nothing when I met you, and I love you with all my soul and all my body as I could never love anybody else; and I cannot think of the possibility of another love. I think I told you something about the relation to my wife. I cannot easily write about this, but if I could only tell you when I was sitting near to you, it would be different, then I could explain it all, it has been rather difficult and complicated. I have a few really good lady-friends, who, I think, care for me, as friends. I still like them, but nothing more, and I am afraid that they interest me much less since I met you, though that is not as it ought to be perhaps, and shows how selfish our feelings often are.

How ridiculous and stupid the general ideas about marriage and sexual morality often are. If you marry and swear that you will be faithful to one man forever whether you love him or not, then it is not only moral to have sexual intercourse with him, but it is immoral if you do not fulfill your duties to him as a wife, and do not give him the sexual satisfaction he needs. If a woman has got no sexual passion, or has no charms so that she is never exposed to any temptations and therefore is what is called virtuous, she is praised as a moral saint, but if a woman is charming, is very attractive and able, and has got lovers, she is condemned as immoral.

(This is really not interesting at all, but I have promised not to tear up anything I have written to you, so let go!)

III

HOW UNFAIR, and how absurd, I am sure that the disposition of the latter one is much nicer, and she has got a better and nobler character. Those sexless, cold, and so called virtuous and disappointed women are often very disagreeable, curious and nasty. But it is really strange how different people (I believe especially women) can be as regards sexual feelings. A doctor I know told me about a woman who had been his patient. She was young and had had several lovers, but she could obtain no real and full satisfaction by sexual intercourse, and this was a great disappointment and caused her much distress and mental depression. Then she spoke to a friend about it, and he thought he could teach her how she could obtain the necessary orgasm, and she decided to take lessons and though she did not care for him, she slept with him every night for a week, and was instructed in all secrets, but it did not help her, she could not get any real pleasure out of it. This is probably a rare case I suppose; but one reason may be, perhaps, that she did not love her partners sufficiently, or that she had begun her experiences too early, and that therefore her erotic imagination could not be sufficiently roused. But nevertheless she wanted to have lovers, she wanted adventures and amusement probably, though they could give her no real pleasure. I have heard about women who have had several children in marriage, but to whom the sexual intercourse was always painful, and they could have no pleasure with other men either.

Saturday, June 1st, evening

IV

MY DEAR DARLING, another letter, (this letter is from May 11th and is the one that seemed to be lost, see later), from you just now, and a wonderful picture, and it makes me just wild and mad with longing. I love your letters, every word; every line in them, how quite remarkably well you write. I never received anything like them before, what a wonderful gift you have to express yourself; and then all the things you say, my darling, you must know that they intoxicate

61

me, give me a wonderful feeling of unspeakable happiness. It must be something like the feeling supposed to be given by the nectar of the gods. And then this picture of you, I adore it. You look like a wonderful strong beautiful Savage. That splendid head, I wish to kiss those eyes and that mouth, kiss it passionately, wildly. And that body! O, I wish those clothes were not there, but I can see the forms underneath, to some extent at least, and those lovely arms which I long to feel round me I embrace, and those splendid, beautifully shaped legs, those delightful thighs. How I wish to feel that lovely soft skin, to take them with my hand. Oh, I long to feel them against my thighs, and be firmly enclosed by them. My eyes follow the beautiful inner lines of those thighs upwards till alas they are covered by the dark clothing before they reach the lap and that lovely delta of black hair, and the entrance to the holy temple of love, and I try to follow the contours of your hips, your waist, your breasts. How beautifully built you really are, and how well that straight body is carried on those legs and those hips. Oh I long to be with you, to have you in my arms, to embrace you wildly, to sleep with you, my dear, dear girl, my darling.

Goodnight. I will dream of you. The last thing my eyes look at is the picture. I press it to my lips, thinking it is your soft, sunburnt skin.

✽ June 1929—Quisling tells Nansen that the Russians had rejected Nansen's Armenian plan. Russia was now in the grip of Stalin, yet Nansen still clung to the illusion of liberalization. Years of effort had been wasted... Nansen had given too much of himself to a lost cause. It may have shortened his life. —RH, *Nansen: The Explorer as Hero*.

Sunday morning, June 2nd

Good morning, Brenda, darling,

I say it to your dear picture, and I kiss you. But I will try to be more sensible now, and answer your letters, at least to some extent, before I begin my work. There are heaps waiting. When I am not very sensible it is not only my fault though, you have to take your share, I hope you do not mind, if you sometimes make me a little mad; you do not wish me always to be sensible, do you? In fact, in one letter you told me not to be sensible, I believe. Nevertheless, I shall try to be it for a little while now. I cannot promise, though, that it will last very long, when I keep on thinking of you, and am not distracted by something else.

There are so many things in your letters which I wish to write about, but how can I get the time? I could write for days, and yet, I have to work, and have only a few days left before I must leave on a trip to Bergen and Northcape and Northern Norway but about that later.

How touching you are to go to the public library to read books for your article about architecture, and then wasting your time by reading books about me instead. I wonder what biography of me it was you found. I do not know of one in English, except by a man called Bain, I believe, but that is very poor, yes, and there is an older one by Nordahl Rolfsen and W.C. Brögger, published by Longmans & Green in 1896 I believe, written before I returned from the "Fram" expedition. The article by T. Hackett [unknown] I do not know, I think. I have to admit, however, that I have a strange reluctance against reading articles about myself; it is a kind of weakness I suppose, or shyness if you like. It is not that I am not pleased if they praise what I have done or written; of course, I like that very much, indeed, especially if you do; nor that I am afraid of criticism, for it is much to be learnt from that; but it is just a reluctance.

How strange that you should just happen to find my book about "Sporting Days etc.," [*Sporting Days in Wild Norway* (1925)] which is one of the few of mine which I have not yet sent, simply because I had to write to England for a copy. I am sending it now though, not because I think it is good (for it isn't, and I wish to be able to improve a great deal of it, I know I could now) but because that too is a part of me, and I wish you to have all of me, or at least as much as possible.

How nice that you liked especially the drawing of the Nymph-haunted pool; I think it is really the best of them; but the reproductions of those illustrations are rather badly printed. The originals are really a great deal better, and there are more of them which were not used, and some of those are among the best. But never mind, it is not so very important. Some time ago I sent you most of my lithographs, etchings, etc. Some of them have been badly printed, especially those of my two daughters Liv on board my yacht and Irmelin (sitting on the terrace outside the house here) are much too dark and hard. I could not be present and control the printing then. But I sent them nevertheless, as I wanted you to get at least some impression of them. And then I sent you as many of my books as I could find copies of, but not the scientific ones, as they would certainly not be worth having, and they are many, and readable only for specialists, especially oceanographers and geologists. I sent you, however, as a sample of my production as a zoologist, a paper on the hermaphroditism of Myzostoma, one of the lowest fishes [Nansen's doctoral thesis: *A Protandric Hermaphrodite (Myxine Glutinosea, L) Amongst the Vertebrates* by Fridtjof Nansen, Bergens Museums Aarberetning, 1888]. (Last year I wrote a new short book about this journey, which is much better, surely, but not published in English.) I actually wrote that paper in Iceland in 1888 lying flat on my belly on the floor of a loft in Dyrafjord, where we lived for two weeks waiting for the ship to take us across to the east coast of Greenland, which I wanted to cross. The drawings for the paper had of course been made in Bergen before I left Norway.

I certainly do not wish you to read all the books I sent you, especially as some of them, especially the books on Russia and Peace, and on Norway and the union with Sweden, are quite out of date, but nevertheless I wish you to have them, as they are closely connected with my activities in some periods of my life. There are some books which I have not sent, because I have not got spare copies of them. They are: "The First Crossing of Greenland" 1890 (out of print and hard to get), "In Northern Mists," 1911, (two vols. W. Heinemann. I will try to get this). "Sporting Days in Wild Norway" 1925 (but written 1916. I am going to send it). Then there is a book about my voyage to Spitsbergen in my little yacht "Veslemøy" in 1912, (A journey to Spitsbergen) [*En Ferd til Spitsbergen*, Kristiana [Oslo]; Jacob Dybwads forlag, 1925], but unfortunately that has not been published in English. I suppose because it contains some scientific chapters, which were too heavy (i.e. too good?) for the general public. But I do wish you could have read it, because there is something in those chapters which I think is really quite worth reading, and I believe you would just like it. But never mind. This was rather much about my literary productivity; if I go on like this I shall never finish this letter, and there are so many things to write about.

You say you have "a longing for exploring, wandering over the world on its loneliest and saddest rims." O, if only we could wander together, my darling, what would it not be, what wonderful happiness, and what great things could we not do when we could complete each other! And you wish to go with me on the north polar expedition. Dear darling, I feel like you, I would not mind what happened as long as we two were together—the end has to come once anyhow, only some immeasurable happiness first. And then I could not bear to think that you should be exposed to any suffering.

Strange, just as I had written this I looked at your letter where you say that you had dinner at the Vanderbilt and watched some people dancing, and you wished you could dance with me. If I do? I would love to, and surely, you dance like a dream, it cannot be otherwise, and it would just be Heaven, to have you in my arms and be carried away. And then I continue to read your letter further, that it would break your heart if I tried to be more sensible, and then you say much more which makes me happier than I can say in words, but bless you for every word! It makes me wild with longing for you, your soul, and your body; but I must try to be sensible just for a little while now and write.

I do wish that you had met my son, Odd, and his wife, Kari. I wish you could see them sometimes, and get on with them. They are really very nice, I think, and I am sure you would like them if you only knew them. That they will like you there can be no doubt, although they will not know what I think of you. What you say about your article on Architecture interests me and I look forward to see it.

What you say about your asceticism seems to show that you have it very much in the same way as I have often had it in my life, and the resemblance is really striking in some respects, when you speak about the training of your body, sleep, etc. You have obviously a strong, violent nature, my darling, you could never be slave to any vice. If you think there is any danger or too much of a thing, you can stop, and so can I. But please be a little careful not to overdo things, with exercise, and training, and work, etc. You can overstrain your body and your brain you know, and then it may take a long time to build it up again.

I speak from sad experience. Be especially careful about sleep. It is certainly true that we can get accustomed to sleep only five hours a night; but it is decidedly much too little, it is unwholesome, and takes too much out of you. Therefore very unwise, and certainly even more so in your age than in mine. You ought certainly to have eight hours sound sleep, it makes you feel healthier and happier, and you work much better. [Most people] are too overtaxed and strained, which perhaps is a danger of American life. Yes, I wish I could sleep with you every night, I would make you sleep, I am sure. I wish you to be temperate in most things at least, but not in love, please, as long as it is love for me.

What you say about dreams coming true if you have faith, is invigorating, indeed, it makes me feel how much you love me. O yes, the future is unknown, happily, and so many things may happen, and it is no good to despair, and I will have hope and confidence, that something good and beautiful is still in store. There is so much in your letter, I wished to talk about if there only was time, about faith and confidence, feeling of guilt and fear etc. You have so many excellent remarks, but another time perhaps. I quite agree with you though.

Your letters are alright and arrive quite safely, and nothing shall happen to them. I have not been able to destroy them yet, though a cablegram sounding very business like and signed Benedict [Brenda's first husband was named William Benedict] would be all right. It is strange that it is just the name of the manager of an office where I have invested some money.

I do not like to think of you walking in those lonely places you speak about where you meet doubtful men who follow you. They may run when you turn enraged towards them, but not always; there are some desperate ones, you know, whom it is difficult to frighten. Couldn't you be a little careful in this respect, when I beg you to? It is all right to risk something for things that are worth it. But, to be raped, or robbed, or murdered by such a worthless brute, is really absurd.

And now your last letter, which I in this moment discover is dated May 11<u>th</u> <u>Saturday</u>, but which I received yesterday after I received yours of the 16th. That explains everything, no letters of yours have been lost, and I am so happy. Fancy if this wonderful letter had been lost, and I had never got it, what a catastrophe! But how strange it is, that it should arrive two days later than the letter <u>mailed</u> six days later. Well, anyhow, I have got it, and I have got your picture, and I am perfectly happy—almost at least, or as much as I can be without you yourself here. How glad I am that you liked my letter and the picture. I was rather doubtful you see, after having got your letters about being sensible, and where you are afraid of having been too ardent. I was not afraid that you would misunderstand, or take it in a wrong way, because I do not really think that you could misunderstand anything I said or did; but you might think it unnecessary, or unwise, and that it was better to be quite sensible, as you said; and then this was not perhaps just the right method.

But now I see I was not mistaken when I thought that perhaps you would like it; and I understand that you are quite as "bad" almost as I am, and I promise you that I will have no hesitation to say anything I think of, or to send you anything, I may perhaps have a few more [photos], I will try to find them and see whether they are worth sending. But I do wish I could have some pictures of you without clothes, especially one like this one in your letter, but I suppose that is difficult for you as you do not develop your pictures yourself. Well, it cannot be helped. I think I could almost make a drawing of you naked after this picture though, but of course that would not be like the real thing, for the photo comes much nearer. And I wanted some better ones of your head as well.

But my dear Brenda, I cannot tell you how deeply moved I am by all you say about my letters, and how much you like them, just those I was afraid would be too hot and irrational for your ironical nature. How wonderful it really is, and how we feel in the same way. I am sure that you cannot like mine better than I like yours. Every one of yours simply works miracles, I feel another being when I read them, and then when I have finished them, and a few hours have gone, I long for the next one, while I recall all you have said in the last one.

It is strange to read what you say about your former husband, but I understand it so well, all your feelings, as I understand everything you write.

I shall not try to discuss now what you say about soul and body, as I will send you a copy of the ms. [manuscript] of my article when I have finished it in a few days, and then you will tell me what you think.

You say that you know nothing about my sexual life, but you "know how much temperament and passion I have and you can tell that I like women very much." Well I think I have already told you something about my feelings, but I wish to tell you everything that might be of interest, as I cannot bear the idea that you do not know every part of me.

That I have temperament and passion is right I hope, at least some. That I like women very much may also be true, but it depends how you understand it. I think my nature really needs a woman to be complete. The fact is that I never had a male friend with whom I could speak much about myself, my feelings, my innermost self, etc. and to whom I could confide my most intimate emotions. That I only could to a woman I really cared for. But I have met with very few such women in my life. The fact is that most of my time I have lived alone, ever from my youth a lonely man. And now, when I am here in my home, I never go out to parties or to friends, refuse all invitations (except to my daughter and son-in-law, and a brother-in-law a few times when they have no parties). And I live in my work, only see wife and daughter at meals, know no women and never see any, live really the life of a hermit, take just a short walk in the wood before dinner at 3:15 p.m. or I may take a walk to the post office about 2/3 of a mile, to mail a letter to you. There you have my life, it is not very exciting, but you have suddenly thrown a new fire into it.

Monday, June 3rd

So far I came yesterday, but I have really much more to say about my sexual life in past years, but will not be time for it now, there is so much work waiting and in a few days I have to leave on a voyage to North Cape (I think I told you?) and shall deliver some addresses to the people in Northern Norway. I am going to Bergen on the 6th evening, shall speak there 7th, evening, and then in various places along the coast northwards as far as Hammerfest [Norway's far north, over 71° latitude]. Shall be back in Bergen June 17th and will be here 18th I suppose.

During this time it may be difficult for me to write to you, I am afraid, as I shall never be alone. My wife and daughter are with me. Please do not become impatient if no letters come for a while, I will do what I can. It is supposed to be a pleasure trip, you understand, with our smartest tourist boat. Do not be nervous about your letters, they will reach me quite safely, although perhaps I shall have to let them wait for my return here, but that will be about the time when you get this. But what wonderful joy to open your letters then, and what letters! Yes, indeed you are right, how dull and lady like, and wan, even the most burning love letters of Mrs. Browning and others become in comparison. Under your words I feel the strong, healthy wild nature, the hot, pulsating blood, the glowing body and soul, and they give me your whole beautiful self.

I look at your picture, I think of all you have said, and I long for you, your soul and body, so intensely, that it is impossible to describe it. If I could pour out my passion for you on paper, you might get really frightened. But my darling, please do not think that I am so very sexual, and that it is merely or chiefly physical sexual passion I have for you. That would be very far from correct. Though certainly

69

it is there, and you would not wish it not to be, still it is only a part, and even a small part, of something much greater, a love, an adoration of your whole being, of your soul and body, of every part of you, and I long to feel, to embrace your naked body and your naked soul, to feel your skin, your flesh, your limbs pressing me, your hot, burning kisses, - your everything—and if I could penetrate into your most intimate, into your most sacred interior I will melt into one with your beautiful soul. O, complete happiness! You are unlike all other women, and I never felt anything like this before, and never can.

I love you!

Fridtjof

I send three small pictures, not good but perhaps you may like to see them, and please destroy them at once if you do not like them, I think I have some better ones, though, from some years ago. I place my picture (standing) opposite yours and think how extremely well we fit each other. I only wish to hug that beautiful body, and lift and press it in my arms. Perhaps though I disturb you too much and rouse your passions, I am sorry. I cannot help it, and I wish you not to forget, you see. This letter has grown very long!

Evening, June 5th, 1929

Brenda, my darling,

A dear, but short letter from you yesterday, with three pictures, two before your wall, and one magnificent acrobatic one. Oh, dear me, what a wonderful body you have, how slim, and athletic; and that body is mine, isn't it? Why can't I take you in my arms, I need it so badly! Oh, darling, I have so much to do, important decisions to take and letters, and notes to write for an "important" speech in Bergen the day after tomorrow, a long meeting with important debates tomorrow, pack, leaving tomorrow night, and I am so dead tired. I only wish to do one thing, and that is to write to you, there is so much I wanted to write about, but I have to wait, and do the most necessary work now, and more tomorrow.

70

Fridtjof Nansen as a toddler.

I

Nansen won worldwide fame for leading the first crossing of the interior of Greenland in 1888, accomplishing the feat on skis. He allowed no line of retreat, proclaiming, "Death or the west coast of Greenland!"

Nansen's ship "Fram," built to withstand great pressure, drifted in the Arctic ice for three years, from 1893-96.

Nansen and Johansen left the Fram with guns, dogs and kayaks, and "dashed" toward the North Pole on foot. They were provisioned for three months. Their dash took 15.

From 1882-88 Nansen was a curator in the zoology department of Bergen Museum. He loved exploring both microscopic and macroscopic worlds.

In his Rectoral address titled "Adventure," given at St. Andrews University in 1926, Nansen told the students, "Privation and suffering are the only road to wisdom."

Nansen and his five children shortly after their mother's death in 1907.

Nansen served as Norway's first Ambassador
to Great Britain from 1906 to 1908.

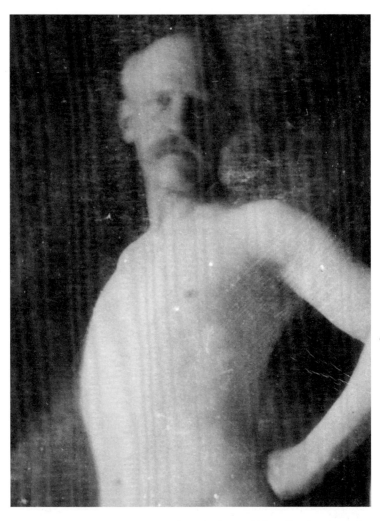

Nansen sent six nude photos of himself to Brenda, urging
her to reciprocate. The photos appear to have been taken earlier
than 1929-1930, the period of their correspondence.

VI

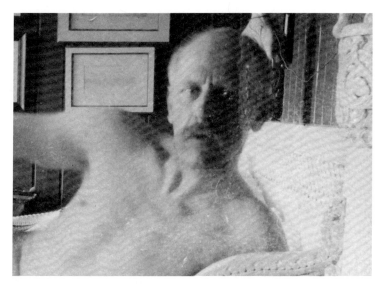

Nansen in his Polhøgda bed, its frame and posts carved in Viking motifs.
Both Eva & Fridtjof's death photos were shot in this bed.

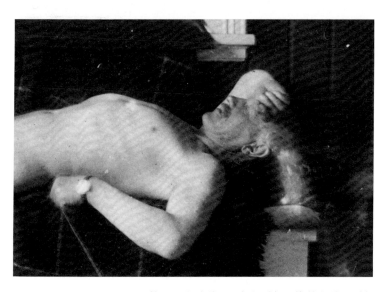

Nansen took these photos himself. Note the cable
leading from his hand toward the camera.

Fridtjof Nansen in New York, 1929.

VIII

I read your article about Freud last night, and liked it very much. How very well you write, and what an excellent brain to be able to absorb and digest all this stuff, which I am sure was new to you when you began to think of the article. I have learnt more about Freud than I ever knew before. But I never agreed with him when he would have sex at the basis of everything. Sex is certainly extremely important but our desire to live is as a rule still stronger. You say that you sent a story too, but that was not in the letter, only the article. Please send it and much more, I long to read it all. I like the pictures of you before the wall, in pajamas, or what it is? You look very nice, but the camera has probably not been quite focused. But those clothes, why could they not be dropped!

You wish to go with me to the Arctic, you wish to go in the Fram for three years, oh yes, what would it not be! And if we never came back, what would it matter, I wish we could remain there.

You say you will write me a long letter about your homosexual friendship. Well you know how I love your letters and I long for them, and as soon as I can I will write you a long letter also. I wish to tell you more about my sexual life, which you said you did not know anything about. But as I told you before I cannot probably write in this voyage, as I shall never be alone, so you must not be impatient if you do not get letters for some time now, I shall not be back here before the 18th. To give you something to read I send you enclosed the end of my article on "My Faith" ["What I Believe," *Forum*, Dec. 1929]. It is not as I would have it, but I have to send it now I suppose as I do not know how soon it is wanted. Therefore, I have sent it to Leach. I wonder very much what you will think about it. You will not like it much perhaps, and not agree. I also send you my little book on sporting in wild Norway. But now I must say goodbye, my Brenda, my darling. You say if you could only hold my hand or just touch my knee, but I could not be satisfied with that, I must have the whole of you, have you in my arms, kiss you, press your breasts, your lips, your thighs, your lap. I love you with all I have, and it is all yours, my darling, how very, very lovely you are.

Fridtjof

Brenda, my dear darling,

I am back this morning from the North, and have found <u>four</u> letters (May 24th with 4 pictures, 28th, 29th, June 3rd with 3 athletic pictures) from you, my dear sweet darling, and I am again bright and happy, and life is lovely sunshine. What a wonderful influence and power you have!! And now I must write to you at once, though there are piles of letters waiting which I have not yet opened, only yours. Poor darling, you have been starving for two weeks when you get this, but during the cruise it was not possible to write a simple line and get it mailed, as there was not one single place to be found, where there was a little peace for oneself. But I think of you and dream of you day and night, that I could, and I would like to have made such a cruise with you, and to have shown you our long beautiful coast from Bergen to North Cape, and the fjords, and valleys, it is really a continuous fairytale the whole voyage, and I know you would enjoy it intensely.

For me it was not merely rest, as I had to make speeches every day at places we came to, and where the people had come from long distances, and there were gatherings of five to six thousand, in one place (Trondheim) even ten to twelve thousand people, who had come to hear your friend. He seems to be quite popular in this country you see. He spoke about politics, which he hates, but it is necessary now to try to make the different parties unite; to make them see the serious danger of the future if they don't; to make them understand the necessity of co-operation in order to overcome our financial difficulties, and to avoid that the communists may get a majority which would ruin the country. A most disagreeable part of it is, however, that the many who are anxious to save the country are pressing your friend to take the lead, and try to make him believe that if he would only hoist his banner and go ahead, they would join under it from all parts of the country. But he will not do it, unless it really becomes absolutely necessary, because he feels he is not fit for it, for all those trivialities of daily life politics and leadership. – But no, this is dull, and surely I was not going to write about politics, which

I really hate, though of course I take a keen interest in the fate of the country, and have had to act on several occasions when I saw that the welfare and the dearest interests of our people were at stake.

But now your letters, they make me long for you more than ever, with soul and body. I wish I could talk with you for hours and days, oh, yes how much I would have to say and to tell you, and I long passionately to have you in my arms, and I feel how much I could give you, and how much you need me just now, in your difficulties. Now I understand how it has all come and developed between you and your friend, [Tomola, Brenda's lesbian lover]; but I cannot agree with you that you are to be blamed for your conduct. As far as I can see you could not easily have behaved otherwise, and without thinking of myself and our relations. I really think you have reason to be glad that it has come to an end, as I hope it has, because otherwise you would have become very unhappy and dissatisfied with yourself.

I understand very well that she is a fine and nice woman, who in many ways has been a good help and support for you, and could have remained so, if the relation had remained "platonic." But I feel convinced that the sexual part of it would in the long run be too unnatural and unsatisfactory for you, so you would not be able to stand it, even if it were you who began to make her make love to you—I believe not so much for your own sake as to please her.

I do not know exactly how women make love to each other, generally, and how they can give each other any sexual enjoyment and satisfaction. I know that in some few and quite abnormal cases, the clitoris may be so abnormally developed that it may be used like a male organ, and give satisfaction perhaps for both lovers; but that is very rarely the case. Otherwise, I suppose the Lesbians press against each other and kiss each other, as is said to be common among the women in the Mohammedan harems, who cannot get sufficient sexual intercourse with their masters. The sexual passion may thus be roused, I suppose, but will hardly ever get the real and full satisfaction. And therefore in the long run it is probably very unhealthy, and makes one nervous and discontented and gives a sad feeling of emptiness.

You say your sexual feelings became very faint after a year, and even at first they were faint, although they may be more roused during the love-making, and although you may get some voluptuous enjoyment out of it your passion is never raised to the refreshing fire, given by a man's embrace, and therefore it seems to me natural that it was a relief to you to hear young married people "discuss earnestly or ribaldly obstetrical details, sexual intercourse etc." I know that the real lesbians have a horror of sexual life between men and women, and think it very nasty. But I do not understand it, and have to satisfy myself with the fact that it is abnormal, and know for certain that you do not feel that way.

You said that you know very little about my sexual life, and I will try to tell you something at least, and should like to tell you everything, if only time permitted, though really there is not so very much to tell. In my young age I was a very virtuous and sexually ascetic young man, and in spite of very strong sexual feelings, I condemned the intercourse of young men with women, and in spite of the most terrible obsessions, I could never touch one of those women or prostitutes, it seemed too ugly, and then probably it was also the fear of the venereal diseases, but not only this fear prevented me. As a young student (19 years) I met a much older good-looking and experienced woman of our high life. It was at her country house where we were shooting. I was a healthy, strong young man, and she fell in love with me and I fell in love with her. I had never kissed a woman before, but she kissed me, and soon taught me what a kiss meant and how to kiss in the most passionate way. I thought it was delightful, and liked her very much indeed, but could not dream of going any further. After a while I began, however, to suspect that she wanted more, she wanted my body. While we kissed I felt her press her body against mine, her lap, her thighs, and I was almost horrified, and though her caresses had made me quite mad, and my love-flesh was swelling, I could not think of anything as wicked as to spoil our "beautiful" relation, and could not respond to her invitation, but withdrew ashamed of myself. And so it went on, and she did what she could, she invited me into her bedroom, she accompanied me to mine, when I went to bed, in order to see whether my bed was well prepared, and we kissed each other but there it ended, she never got more.

Then for years I never kissed or touched a woman. I came to Bergen 21 years old, in 1882, as curator of the zoological Museum, and I lived in the house with some very nice people, husband and wife without children. [Pastor Wilhelm Holdt and his wife Marie.] We were very good friends, and the landlady (I think about 15 years older than I) was charming. After I had lived there with them for nearly a year and a half, I went on a trip on skis across the mountains, which I have described in the book: "Sporting Days in Wild Norway" (the first story) I sent you last. When I was leaving in the morning (January 28ᵗʰ 1884) the landlady had turned out to give me breakfast before I left. But when I said goodbye, she was so very nice, implored me not to be too reckless in the mountains and to take care of myself, and she looked at me in such a charming, anxious manner that I was deeply touched and could not withstand the temptation but kissed her, just touching her lips, and she did not withdraw but rather responded I thought, and I went away happy, and not ashamed of myself. When I came back, we were the same good friends as before, or perhaps a little warmer, and so it remained. But long after that, perhaps half a year or more, there was a fire in Bergen in the night, and as usual on such occasions the town was warned by canon-shots (as fire signal), and the bells of the churches were ringing solemnly. We all three turned out and met in the sitting-room, and while the husband went out into the town to see what was going on, she and I remained waiting. She was a little anxious, and she looked so charming in that dim, uncertain light, and in her light dress. I got a feeling of protection, and could not withstand the temptation. I kissed her. She did not object, but kissed me again, it was so wonderfully sweet, and we kissed each other again and again. I took my arms round her, and she did not withdraw, our kisses became quite hot. I could see part of her bosom under the nightgown, I could not help it, my hand would glide down and take round one of those lovely swelling breasts, she did not object, but

75

kissed me, and the hand, pressed it and it felt for the first time the breast of a woman, a wonderful sensation and it felt the charming little nipple, and it went across and found the other breast, and she let it willingly all happen, and even let down the nightgown a little to help me. It was simply wonderful, but after a while the hand would glide further down to feel her body and her belly; but then I did not dare to go any further, and there it stopped, and at last the husband came back, the fire was local and did not threaten the town (which was built of wood) and we parted and went to bed again, but I dare say I did not sleep much more that night. After that event, we often kissed each other, but nothing more happened, and I considered it to be quite impossible that such a thing could happen, that I should really embrace her; until at last, of course, we could not help it any longer, and I found the way to her lap, but the sensation when first I felt her hair, was something indescribable. I was, however, so perfectly stupid and inexperienced, that she had to help me and get me into her arms, etc. That was the first woman I ever had. After that we had naturally much intercourse, and it was a very happy time for me, and for her too. Her husband had not much sexual feelings, and therefore did not give her much, so she needed very much more for satisfaction, as she was a healthy woman with passion. She was a very nice and good woman too, with a kind heart, and did much good work for the poor people. She loved me really I believe, but at the same time she had a kind of motherly feeling for me, too, and thought that I really needed to have her, and that she did a good thing by satisfying my sexual passion, and that celibacy was not good for me, which it certainly was not, and that she protected me against the temptations of bad women. That she did, indeed, and I cannot be grateful enough to her for her real goodness, and I cannot but think that she did the right thing, she became a better and more natural person by it, and my whole existence was certainly much improved. She did not do any harm to her husband either, as he was, as I said, sexually so indifferent, that it really could make no difference to him, I believe that he really was of a somewhat homosexual nature without knowing it himself, at least some of his family (father and sister) were homosexual. He was a very nice and good man, though, clergyman, and has done more good for suffering people and for prostitutes, etc. He lives still, 84 years old, but she is dead several years ago. He adores me, and thinks I am a great man.

In that manner I was saved from troubles of all kinds, and lived in Bergen till 1888 when I went on my expedition across Greenland. When I returned I married my first wife [Eva Sars], who was a remarkable woman, an unusually gifted singer, every fiber of her was music, and an intellect which is very rare. She loved me passionately and I loved her more than I can say, but still when I proposed to her I had to tell her first that I was obliged to go on an expedition across the North Polar regions, I did not know for how many years. She wanted to marry me nevertheless, but made me promise to take her with me. I thought, however, that if she got a child, she would not go.

The first child (a boy) came three months too early, the second child (a splendid boy) was killed during the birth, which was very difficult. I was perfectly miserable. But then came a daughter, my eldest one [Liv], alright and that settled it, she no more thought of going, and I sailed half a year afterwards. After more than three years I came back, three hard years for her, but she had her music and her child. Had given many concerts, and very successfully! Then we met and were perfectly happy.

June 20th, morning
So far I came yesterday, and here you have me again, and now I must finish this and have it mailed after midday, in order that you shall not wait longer than necessary for a letter. I feel tired, I do not know why, but I long for you more than ever, long to be with you in some lonely place far, far away from everything, just you and I!! What a wonderful rest it would be, just to lay my head on your breast, or in your lap. You ask whether I am musical, I cannot say that I really am, as I cannot perform anything, but I love music, there is nothing that can stir my feelings like it and no language that can express them so wonderfully.

77

But I should try to finish my story: After my return from the Fram expedition [in Aug. 1896] my wife and I had a happy life. Then there came, however, some clouds. I flirted with some ladies, it was not very serious, as I loved my wife above everything and adored her; but she suffered very much by seeing me flirt with others, and it was really wicked of me when I knew that she would suffer by it, but I suppose it is the spirit of the explorer which longs to explore new lands. But as I said it was not really serious, and was very little compared with the deep love I had for her. Then she died in 1908 [sic. Dec. 9, 1907] and I was perfectly miserable, stunned and broken down for a long time. What has happened after that is really not so very much. The relations to my present wife [Sigrun] dragged on all that time, until she at last left her husband [Gerhard Munthe] and I thought it right to marry her about ten years ago. Here at home I always lived the life of a hermit, working in my tower and never seeing anybody, a most unsociable and impossible man, whom now at last people as a rule leave alone, as he is known to be inaccessible. So you understand there is no possibility of any flirtation here. When I travel I meet occasionally nice women, and there may perhaps be a little flirtation, but nothing very serious. I will not say that I am a saint, but I am really not so very bad either, and there has been nothing which I think is worth mentioning, or which I think would be of much interest to you.

You say that you think I, like Goethe, need women. It may be true perhaps. But still my sexual feelings are not so strong that I cannot control them. I can give you an example. I remember one summer in Bergen, when my hostess (and mistress) and her husband were away during six weeks I think, and I was alone in our house with a maid. I was accustomed to the regular intercourse with my mistress then, and this separation was painful, and I suffered much. The maid was a nice strong, healthy peasant girl, and she slept in the room next to my bed-room. It was therefore, hardly unnatural, that in the nights when longings made it difficult to sleep, I began to think of her, and some evening I proposed to her that she should let me come into her bed.

She got horrified, and answered: "What would the clergyman say?" I meant (said) he could not say anything as he would not know. She seemed to hesitate and refused reluctantly. When in the night I came to her door it was locked inside, I knocked and implored her to open I would certainly not do her any harm. She said she was afraid, but opened nevertheless, and when I came in she was again lying in her bed. I laid down alongside her, while she was lying still without moving, and without saying a word, pressed my body against her side, her thigh and hip, and became naturally very hot. After having lain thus for some time, I laid my hand over her lap and then she trembled all over without moving or speaking though, and I, in my stupidity, did not understand that it was voluptuous passion, but thought she was afraid of what might happen, and assured her that I would not do her any harm, and should not touch her, and I took my hand away without ever feeling her trembling lips. I remained quiet only pressing my lap against the side of her thigh, until at last the end came. Then I rose, but as I went out, she said with a very sad voice: "How is that, do you get enough only by lying beside a woman?" I answered that I would not do her any harm, she really seemed to be very disappointed. The next morning when I came down to breakfast, I felt very much ashamed of myself, and said nothing, hardly dared to look at her. A few nights later, I could not stand it any longer, but again came in to her, and now the door was not shut, and she did certainly not object to my coming, and I again lay down beside her. I said that I was afraid I disturbed her, but I could not help it, I had too strong feelings. She said she understood that, but that she had not been able to sleep the other night after I had made her so mad, and then left her. I was sorry, but now I did not even touch her lap, but lay beside her, till again the end came, and I left her. But later in the night I again became too passionate, and came in to see her again. I asked her whether she had slept, and she said yes, she was more accustomed to it now, though obviously she thought that I did not behave as I ought to by not giving her what she actually needed. But I lay down beside her again, and nothing more happened than before.

I do not think I came, and after some time my hostess came home again. But strange to say, I always repented bitterly afterward, that I did not do more, and did not embrace the girl. It would certainly have given her satisfaction and made her happier; and it was really a mean thing not to do it; but at the time I thought it might make life more difficult for her, and it would disturb her; but if so I ought of course not to have approached her, as my behavior was decidedly not nice at all. But nevertheless it shows that my sexual feelings did not make me quite reckless, especially as it was of course a great temptation to try to experience how she would behave under my caresses, and how she would take the whole thing, and it would be quite a new and unknown sensation with a maiden. Things like this have happened several times later in life, when I did not grasp the opportunity, and withstood temptations for fear of doing harm. I believe in every case it was a mistake, and stupid, and I repent very much; but as it is, and it proves anyhow that the feelings do not always run away with me, though it is nothing to be proud of, certainly not!

But here I have to stop, as I see I must go to the post office with this. There are so many things in your letters, and so much I have to say, but that must wait till later. Goodbye Brenda, my darling, I love you and long for you desperately.

Fridtjof

June 22nd, 1929, evening

Dear Brenda, my darling,

I have been so strangely depressed these last days, in spite of your inspiring letters which I got on my return three days ago, and which made me so very, very happy. I suppose it is a little overstrain of the brain. But in this moment came your wonderfully hot letter of June 7th (in which you say that you have just got my letter telling that I had got home and found letters from you), and a mighty wave of happiness, and fire, and passion, and virility floods my whole existence, my heart, my soul, my body, and I feel that you are near me, you are here in my tower, I will see you, if only I dare to turn round. And I will take you in my arms, and I will kiss you passionately, and will press and embrace you wildly, and you will—well you will be simply wonderful, and let me understand that you love me with every fiber of your body and your soul. I cannot thank you enough for all the nice things you say, your love, your passion, every word. I look at your last pictures, which I did not get time to mention in my last letter two days ago. I love them; they make me see you in your beauty, and feel you so near, the athletic ones are splendid, what a splendid beautiful body you have, I can see the forms, the muscles, the lovely arms, the strong, well-shaped thighs, the buttocks, and I wish I could just lift you in my arms as you are sitting there on the ground, and press you against my body, and put my hands round those buttocks and thighs and in between them, and I wish you were quite naked, without those "stupid" clothes. And I can see your face on those pictures too, it is quite good, with a nice expression (on the two standing and sitting on the ground) but not quite as I remember you. This is also the case with the face on those two (standing and sitting) of the sailor boy, though very pretty indeed, and I like them, but the fourth of you, leaning against the wall, I love; that is just as I remember you, that beautiful face with an expression of wandering thoughts, the whole attitude with the arms and legs crossed, oh yes, I love, love you my dear, dear girl, and mistress and queen, and I wish I had you here in this moment, but I would kill you with my love.

Midsummer eve, June 23rd, morning
A lovely morning, the sun is shining, after a wet refreshing night, and glittering in the rain drops on the leaves, the roses are in blossom, soon there will be an undulating sea of red and yellow roses in the garden, and it is midsummer eve, and tonight there will be bonfires in every direction and fire-works, and the youth will rejoice, and I will see it all here from my tower; but you are not there, and my thoughts will travel across the ocean and find you, my darling, and I know they will meet your thoughts on the way.

But now your letters, there are so many things to talk about, and there are now five of them which I have not yet answered; so I am afraid it will only be little I can cover, I read them over and over again, and they make me wild with longing, and still fill me with happiness. You say so many wonderful things about your love, your feeling, your passion, that I cannot express in words the gratitude I feel, the warm, wonderful feeling of exaltation and buoyancy it gives me; perhaps I could make you understand a little of it, if I had you here, if I had you in my arms, and could melt into one with you.

Yes I should wish to go on writing you the whole day, and all my work seems so trivial compared with it; as you say it gives a sense of existence, reality. Still at the same time I have a kind of feeling that you would not like me so much if I do not do my work properly.

I look at your letters to see what it was I wished to answer, but every time I get fascinated and spellbound by the wonderfully charming things you say -- for instance, how we would sit and what we would do, when we could talk for hours and days -- and I forget everything, only just want to be suffocated by you. Bless you for all you say about our first meeting when I came out to your house.

I am so glad that you saw my son [Odd], and liked him, and I feel sure you will like her [Kari], too, and I do hope that you have met, and that they have been with you, they would love it, and it is so very nice of you to wish them to come. But I do not think we need to pity them, they are very happy, and she is very proud of her baby, and is a very good, and wise mother, I think. But I do pity your young brother and his wife, a gloomy, mother-in-law that is trying indeed, and is certainly much worse than to be "hard up and no chance for any gaiety or high life." I know that if I could only live with you, I would care for nothing else, just work and you do your work, and we two together, and the rest of the world nothing, fancy only we two together the whole day and the whole night! But you are young, I must not forget, and you need a little more, it would not be good for you to be cast away from everything too long. But you need not be afraid, they would not be jealous of you, they would easily understand how much you could give me, or at least some part of it. Yes, he is a very nice boy; he is like me in some things, but in others he is like his gifted mother, and that I like. He is really gifted, but has perhaps too many strings on his bow.

Oh yes, how wonderful it would be to get a son with you. Fancy what possibilities. But of course, whatever you say, I would wish him to be like you, and only in a few certain things like me, just a few qualities worth having. What a splendid specimen of our race he would be, and what great things he could do, and how happy and proud we would be, though I would not live to see him grow to a man, but would be happy to leave him in your hands.

I think I did already speak about your love affair, in my last letter, so I will not say more about that now. But how like you to say that you like to know all kinds of people "bad people, dirty people, nymphomaniacs, fools, nincompoops, as well as smartly fashionable attired and epicene ladies and gentlemen." You like to know and experience all sides of human nature. It is your spirit of adventure and exploration, and certainly there is no more interesting field to explore, and there are always new lands and new mysteries to be discovered. This is it also that makes me feel that I can speak to you about everything, and wish to hide nothing, knowing that you will understand it all. But the most beautiful part of it is that, though you know so much, and have had so many experiences, you can feel so intensely, so passionately, and love so wholly, with your whole soul and your whole body; to me you are like a young healthy girl, a maiden [Nansen named his yacht "Veslemøy", literally "Little Maiden" in Norwegian.]

Yes, I do like your wild, shaggy hair, which you mention in your letter of May 29th, it makes you look like the savage I love, and whom I saw in the picture you sent me before, it is the daughter of nature with the wild primary passions, reckless and wonderful, oh, I love you my dear girl, more than I can possibly say.

But please do not be so gloomy about your broken affair, and do not take it so much to heart and be so depressed about it. I am sure it could not be helped, it would have come to an end of some kind anyhow, and certainly you are not to be blamed for it. It was unnatural to you and impossible in the long run, whatever you say. And then remember that time cures everything (except our love though!). But you must not do too much of your exercises, and do not get too thin, I am afraid it is not good for you. I know from experience that it may reduce your brain power too, and make you feel tired or depressed, and then one has to be careful not to work too hard. I had a friend who was entirely ruined that way, so be careful about yourself, my darling, and do not tax your beautiful body and your beautiful soul too much at the same time.

You say in your letter of June 3rd that I must not be depressed. No I will not, and I am not when I think of you, and I always think of you, so I do not see really why I should feel depressed. Is it because sometimes you seem so far away. Oh yes, I know how very, very much you can give me, and how, as you say, when I talk with you revelation after revelation would come to me, my dear darling. Oh you write so beautifully about it all, about my coming in to you that night, and how much you love me, and feel that all I have is yours, bless you for it my dear, dear girl. I only wish I could have you in my arms to let you feel how true it is.

You say that it is a strange thing, that in each succeeding letter I seem to know you better. Well I really feel as if I know every part of you; it is because I always think of you, perhaps, and then I love you so much, and then you have such a wonderful ability in your letters to let me see into your interior and make me feel your most intimate feelings. So we really, and fully belong to each other; and I feel perfectly confident that we complete each other in a marvelous manner, and if only we could live together, I could never let you go again even for a short time, so you would have to give up all hope of freedom and independence, I am afraid, as I would only too willingly give up mine. We would be together every day and every night, and I could never get too much of you, I know, -- never get enough. And you say to give me consolation, rest and renew me, that is "what your lap, arms, breast, entire body is for, my place of renewal," yes indeed so it is, and you say further more "since you have felt my neck, and my breast and my arms and thighs and body," you "long to go with your melancholy and apprehension to the shelter of my arms and body" etc. Oh my dear, dear darling!!

How strange and very nice that you "slept with some wedding cake under your pillow and dreamed of me" "with such realistic transported passionate realism," it makes me feel awfully happy.

You say that "Goethe had a great need of women, terrific, all-pervading sexual feelings and so have" I, and "therefore I am to love you as passionately as I can" (I think you could not ask for more than there already is) and I "am to consummate my passion for you as soon as I can and as long as I feel it for if I do it will give my life, my work a force and a vitality that it cannot have otherwise." Indeed that is true even more so than you can imagine, and bless you for saying it. As to my all-pervading sexual feelings I have already told you something about that in my last letter I think.

You are touching, indeed to say that "even if I should love somebody else and not you" I am to consummate my passion for this somebody "and with your blessing always." Oh my darling how like you, but you need not be afraid of that, I cannot love somebody else after having met you. But I do agree with what you say about jealousy etc. Of course I do wish to have you for me alone, and I would be sorry if I knew that you had another lover, but I believe I could not love you less for that, and I could not be really jealous, until you yourself told me the contrary. I would believe that you still loved me above everything, and that the other relation was simply because your passion needed some satisfaction. But all you say about this that you could not accept any love but mine, and that I won't lose you, and have you now as if you shared my room with me, and slept with me every night fill me with joy and pride and happiness. And so you would think about me too in a similar case, I am sure, would you not? Though you do wish to have me for you alone, not only my soul but also my body.

I wonder how you really felt after Gaby left you, and you

85

were alone, and how you feel now. I think of it that is just during this time that you will get no letters from me to cheer you up (as I really understand that they do, thank God!) for nearly two weeks, and that makes me miserable, and perhaps you will already have left for Minneapolis, when my letter (June 20ᵗʰ), sent after my return, reaches Stamford. I do not think that Gaby begins to discard you, my darling, and "use you only for clothes, meals, and consolation." I think she never will, and will long back to you. But of course children like variation, and to see new things, and new surroundings. I suppose they would not be children if they did not.

Well darling I will not think of time and "the last act" and all that, but just be happy because you love me, and your passion for me does "heighten every moment of my existence" and makes me "light-headed and tranquil" and also incandescent and glowing!!

You speak of the last picture of me in the second volume of "Farthest North." I suppose you mean the picture of me before Jackson's hut at Cape Flora. Do you see how fat and heavy I was then? I had increased 25 pounds during that journey after I left the Fram; it was the life in the winter hut that did it I suppose.

How very nice of you to have asked Odd and Kari and the baby to come. I do hope they did, and I long to hear how you liked them. I cannot tell you what joy it gives me to think that they are with you, and that you can become friends.

You say that you are not handsome enough in those pictures, and that if only I were there you could show me a beauty. Oh yes, my darling, don't you think I know it, the most beautiful girl I ever saw, with a heavenly, sweet face, and a perfect body without any clothes, and I would take her in my arms, and kiss her and suffocate her with my love.

And now I come to your last letter of June 7ᵗʰ. How happy I feel that my letter after I came home from Germany could give you so much joy. Oh, you should only know how poor an expression my letters give for what I really feel!! I was of course much interested to read what you tell me about your confessions to your sisters [Anne and Elsa] and [sister-in-law] Julie. I wonder what they think about it all, and what they think about your "admiration" for me, although they do not know how much it really means? I suppose they will have their thoughts about it, and will find out, though. But I think it is wise to be cautious, though I hate it, as it might make it easier in the future, and after all it does not really concern others; and if they get to know in Minneapolis it may reach this side, and cause some trouble perhaps; it is really strange how people take keen interest in such things. I do not care a rap, the only thing I am afraid of, is that difficulties should be thrown in our way. It will certainly be much easier for us in the future as long as nobody knows. Do you really think that your father would like it if he knew how much we feel for each other? How very nice, I like him so very much, and admire him; but still it is better he should not know, I think.

Your description of your composer [Dimitri Mitropoulos] and your dinner with him, is most amusing. I can see you, lovely and pretty, with that little man, "with a deep rich theatrical voice and a very broad soft waistline," and I think I can almost hear your conversation and his wonderful confession, which he thought was very bold.

How nice it is that after your long discussion with Anne of homosexuality versus heterosexuality, you have made such a strange discovery as to marriage between men and women and that you think it might be "possible to have such a strong physical bond, that they become quite free," and you feel, "that if you lived with me, slept in my arms every night (as I am sure you would), yet you would have none of that thwarted, caged feeling that you have always had with others." Well, I feel quite confident you would not, and I would not allow you to, and the bond would be too strong for that, surely; and besides I would have too much love and too great a veneration for your beautiful independent soul, and all these other feelings, doubts, restiveness and all the rest would dwindle into trifles. There would only be the one great feeling of love and adoration. We need each other and complete each other, as no other people can do.

You write again and again about your friend, and I understand how much it really worries you. I think you need me badly, my darling, and oh, if only I could be there to help you, and chase those dark shadows away. Oh yes, if I could be there in this minute.

It has become evening now, and the bonfires will soon be lighted, but all my thoughts go to you, Brenda, my darling. You say I must never be sad. How can I, when I think of you? I see you in your bed, in all your lovely beauty, you smile and open your arms. Oh, your dear lovely head with the black shaggy hair, your beautiful face, with the dreamy expression, your round breasts, your wonderful body, your delightful lap with the black hair, your splendid thighs, your well-shaped calves and feet. Oh yes, how wonderful you are! Come, let me feel your lovely skin, let me caress your body, your breasts, your hips, your thighs, let me feel how you tremble with passion. Come, come, open your arms and your thighs and take me into you in a wild, wonderful embrace. I kiss, kiss you, lips glued against lips, I suffocate you, I sink deep into you, your thighs and arms round me, I am drowned in you. Oh, my Brenda, ...you give me new vitality, new strength, new buoyancy, your joy of living, your spirits flow from your soul and your body into mine, you make me a new and better man. And I sleep in your arms the whole night, and in the morning we rise happy and bright to a new day, and we do great things, because we love each other so unspeakably, and stimulate and complete each other.

Your Viking Fridtjof

Evening, June 24th, 1929

I do not dare to look this through as there might be too much I wanted to alter and express better, or strike out. You shall have it as it is, you understand everything I know, and will take it as it is meant, and never misunderstand, and you know that I love you, <u>soul</u> and body.

Wednesday evening, July 3rd, 1929

Brenda, my girl, my mistress, my everything!

It seems an eternity since I wrote to you (have forgotten now, but was it the 23rd and 24th?). Would have written every day, but hoped for a letter from you first, thought I would wait just one day more then it would come, but every mail disappointed me, and I began to become a little uneasy, had anything happened with your letters?

In the mean time I worked hard. I am writing a new book, [*Through the Caucasus to the Volga*, Allen & Unwin, 1931], a continuation of my book about Armenia [*Armenia and the Near East*, Allen & Unwin, 1928]. It is a description of my journey across Caucasus, to Daghestan, where I had a short stay, and then the voyage across the Caspian Sea and up the Volga. It will not be much of a book, quite short I think, but I have to get it written down, else it would not give me peace. I will send it to the press here very soon, but whether there will be an English edition I do not know. I do wish it though, as otherwise you cannot read it, and what use of writing it then?

But then, oh happiness! This morning came a delightful letter from you, my darling, written on June 17th. And I was transformed, would write this evening, and work steadily during the day, So I did, but with the mail this evening came another glorious letter from you, written on June 14th and 15th, and I am more than transformed. I am simply mad and wild with longing for you my wonderful girl! So lovely, so passionate, so glorious you are! But you almost frighten me, my darling; you say my letters are like a drug, they make you so passionate, "but then a worse craving than ever begins." Is it perhaps wrong of me to write you such letters? Do they disturb you too much? But oh, I cannot help it, I must give vent to my feelings, for I love you so intensely, body and soul. And now, by reading your wonderful, passionate letter, it is as if I have you here, as if I ...am drowned in you, melt into one with you; it is as if our whole life, our souls, our thoughts, our dreams, our bodies are concentrated wholly into our love-organs, and everything else disappeared, forgotten, you and I are no more we, we are one, in another world. Oh, yes, my wonderful girl, how glorious, how perfect you are in every way, and how wonderfully strong, and sound, and passionate – no, that is such a poor word, but I cannot find a better one, to express that which I really feel about you;

but I love you so unspeakably, so over all words.

But how can I answer the many, many things in your letters, I want to speak about. I have so much to say, it would make a book; I must, however, try not to be too long, but get this sent in order that you shall not wait too long, especially as this letter will probably have to travel all the way to Minneapolis, I understand. I am so very glad that you really liked my article about "my faith," I was much afraid that you would not like it, would think it too dry and business-like. I suppose many people will be shocked by such "materialism," though of course I cannot admit that is more materialistic than the ideas of those who at any cost will have something more out of existence. I think they are rather materialists and greedy ones. But never mind. I have not heard from [Henry Goddard] Leach or the "Forum" [magazine] yet, and whether that was what they expected.

You speak about your brother Rolf that he is "so remote and so lonely that the very first girl that holds his hand" – etc. And you ask whether that is Norwegian? Yes I think it is in a way, really. The Norwegians have perhaps a tendency to be more sentimental, and less business like than Americans, in this respect. It struck me what an American friend of mine once said about his daughters. "Why make these young people read poetry? It only gives them dreams, which they will discover cannot be fulfilled, when they learn to know real life." I think we have perhaps too many dreams for practical life. I know, I have had, and it has often been hard to get away from them.

It is really strange that you should say that I am perhaps too conscientious. Yes that is just what I am; and you seem to know me almost better than I myself. And by God, how much you could help me, my darling, what a wonderful thing if only we could be together and we could always help and complete each other!!

Thursday morning, July 4th, 1929

I must try to send this letter with the mail now. Next week I will go to the mountains with my daughter Irmelin. There I will be quiet and undisturbed for some weeks. I will write peacefully and finish my book and do other things too. My daughter will paint, and in the afternoons we will go fishing trout, along the rivers and lakes, and get exercise, a healthy life, which gives new strength and peace. But your letters will have to travel two days more, before they reach me, alas, and then from Minneapolis, they will need still more. But as you say, I will also try to write shorter letters but oftener. You are afraid that your "letters may be a hackneyed repetition of" how you love me. How absurd, they are just you, as you feel, wonderful, giving new strength, new hope, new will, new courage, new buoyancy, new joy in life, new happiness! Can real love, passion ever be hackneyed?

Oh yes, darling how well I remember that Friday afternoon when your father was with you, and how I regretted afterwards that I did not come. But you see, I thought (as I think I told you in the phone in a way) that I would not be able to see much of you then, and I wished to be with you alone, and you spoke about seeing your sister too I believe, and then it would be so complicated I thought, and I did not get time to think in that phone. But dear me, how I repented my stupidity afterwards, when it was too late. I could not ring you up again, how would that look. Yes, how stupid one can be. Damn it!

How strange that already last year, you should have thought of me when your father and Mrs. Dale spoke about me, and that you even had such ideas as to cut her out with your wonderful brown eyes.

I cannot tell you how happy it makes me to think that you like my son, and Kari, and Marit so well, and what a glorious time they have had with you. How very, very nice that you seem to understand Odd so well. Yes, he is a good boy, and quite intelligent; and he likes to argue—perhaps a little too much. I am sure they like you very much, how could they help it, being with you so long? But I have not heard from them yet. How strange that Kari did not like my wife because she is too jealous. It is true, and it is a very unfortunate tendency, it ruins so much, especially for those poor people themselves. I was struck indeed when I came into your father's house and saw that picture, [of a young Sigrun Munthe, Nansen's second wife, painted in 1886 by Gerhard Munthe, and acquired by Brenda's father, Andreas

Ueland], which I had not seen for more than forty years when it had just been painted. It is painted by her husband Munthe, who then got engaged to her that same summer when it was painted. It is a good picture. How very strange that you should have grown up with it! But she is not a bit like you.

How very nice your sister Anne is, taking so much interest in me that she even writes to others about me. I liked her awfully much.

I think you are quite right, our gloomy moods certainly are very often our guts; drinking or smoking too much have certainly such an effect upon me, or also too much work and overstraining the brain. But it is refreshing to read your frank statement of the facts. But, my darling, your account of your run to the train makes me a little uneasy, you are wonderful, I know, and you certainly have a splendid heart. But still you are not quite young any longer (fortunately for me), and you know that just in that way the heart may easily be overstrained. I know it from my own experiences though I had an unusually good heart. And many strong people have been ruined that way; it is really extremely dangerous, so please be careful, for my sake. To miss a train is no great affair (as a rule) but to ruin your heart?

It gives me joy to read what you say about my poor drawings, though certainly they do not deserve it. I only wish I had time to do some drawings now, for you. How very much better they would be.

Please do not waste much time on those books of mine which you mention, none of them are really worth it. But you might rather read the book, (*Sporting Days in Wild Norway*), which I sent later. There may be a few things in that which would interest you. I tried to get "In Northern Mists" (2 vols. History of early exploration) but unfortunately it is out of print.

The letter you write about, which was thought to be lost, turned up all right; but I have written you about that before, and I shall not now begin to discuss jealousy and all that. I could have so much to say. But you need not be afraid. I will not give you any reason; because I love you, my darling, love you above everything.

But now I must go with this letter to the post office, and will write more later. I wish I could take you in my arms, press you violently, kiss you and forget everything else.

Fridtjof

Sunday evening, July 7th, 1929

My dear Brenda, my dear darling,

Now I am alone here in the house, all are away, and then I must write to you. My last letter was written 3rd and 4th. I am sitting here in my tower, a lovely evening, and I have been working all day. I will tell you something you have never heard before: I love you, and I long for you, desperately. Fancy if you were here what would we do, and what would we not do? Well I know something we would do, but will not tell you, though perhaps you know. Oh yes, I would take you in my arms and kiss you, my sweetheart, and you would sit on my lap and hug me, and I would press you, and I would tell you many nice things, and I would look into that beautiful face into those wonderful eyes, and I would feel your whole body, and your soul, and your everything, and I would be really and wonderfully happy.

You say in your last letter: "it delights me and makes my heart beat with wonderful excitement to think how dangerous this all is, -- your letters and mine leading us into such an abyss of love, it seems quite bottomless." Yes it is true, my darling, it is dangerous indeed, I have thought of it, not for my sake, but for yours. But what can we do? We cannot help it now I am afraid; and should we, if we could? Make life poor and miserable? I think of you however, have I a right to plunge into your life like this? I disturbed your relation to Tomola, that I do not regret though, on the contrary, I am sure that was a really good thing, but further? You are young, I am old, have you really considered how old I am? and how many years I have left? May I intrude and disturb your possibilities of making a good plan for your life? Well it is no good talking of that now I suppose, I cannot preach with much conviction, and you will not listen I know. You ask: "Do you ever think darling that when you <u>do</u> see me and I undress for you and you lift me up and the whole of my body is in your possession...

well you might not ever be able to leave me again?" Yes, true, it is very dangerous; but that is happiness, one has to run risks, I suppose, to obtain it, and one never knows what the future may bring. But fancy to see you undress for me, how wonderful it would be. It is strange, but I cannot remember how it was. Why? But to see you remove your clothes piece after piece, and your lovely body gradually appears, until the last piece drops, and you are standing there in all your naked glory, oh wonder! ...And we are wonderfully happy, till we get too passionate and go to bed. And in the morning we rise wonderfully fresh, and we talk and inspire each other, and we work, and we criticize each other's work, and we have a glorious time, till the night comes again and we sleep in each other's arms; but hardly know what is most wonderful night or day?

Had a letter from Kari [Kari Nansen: born Hirsch (1903-1985). Married Odd Nansen in 1927. Marit, eldest child, born in 1928.], she is perfectly thrilled with the wonderful time she and Odd and Marit and Signe had with you, and she likes you so much (as I was sure she would of course) and thinks you are "awfully sweet" and very unusual. I do hope they will see more of you.

Yes indeed you are right, there is certainly no woman in the world who would cherish my thoughts, wishes, aspirations, as tenderly and understandingly as you do; but as I think I have said before I feel also that I have much to give you, which I think nobody else could give you better!

I had a letter from Henry Leach. To my astonishment he likes my article (on my Faith) and says it is just what they want. It reminds him, he says, "of the voice out of the whirlwind in the Book of Job. It is charged with starlight and woman's eyes." What woman's eyes I wonder? There can only be one, do you know her? But he does not know. The plan now he says is to publish my paper second in the series, Bertrand Russell in September and mine in October [sic, Dec. 1929].

In your last letter you say much about courage, which I think is very good, and it agrees with views I have held, though not so clearly expressed. When I look back upon life it is really strange, what I most regret and repent are the lost opportunities when the body, the instincts, the "flesh" was willing and courageous enough, but the brain cowardly held back, and the opportunity was not grasped.

Well, the brain has been trained to warn us against danger and bad consequences, and then it overdoes it, and we become too timid. Courage, as you say, is an essential quality, whilst goodness is so vague, and what is it really? So many different things—some good and some bad. But courage is not foolhardiness, though it may be recklessness. I have so much to say about these subjects, I long to discuss them with you, my darling, while you sit on my lap and hold my hand, and your other arm round my neck. I kiss you goodnight my dear, dear girl and mistress,

Fridtjof

Thursday evening, July 11th, 1929

Dear Brenda, my darling,

Yesterday a new delightful letter from you—can you possibly imagine how happy your wonderful letters make me? Always so refreshing, to the point, no beating round the bush, and filled with love, and feeling, and passion. Oh yes, my darling, you are a wonderful creature, and you are mine, my dear, dear girl, my mistress. But I am not going to write much today, only some lines in order that you shall not wait for a letter in vain (I sent the last one July 7th), and as I am going to the mountains in a day or two, when my daughter comes back (perhaps tonight), there may pass some days before I can write to you again; and alas, the letters will take a few days extra from the mountains, this is very sad, and still more so because your letters will also take some days more. But it cannot be helped. I have been and am working hard, I should finish this book about (the) Caucasus; but then there are so many letters to answer, (damn it they are the curse of existence—except those from a certain person) about the polar expedition and all its difficulties, and then about work for the Refugees and their difficulties, and then many other things which they want me to do and

95

which I do not wish to. It is really ridiculous to think of it how much precious time we waste on correspondence which is really no good and quite unnecessary at least for oneself. But this is I suppose what is called social duties. Come let us go to another planet!! or at least to Tahiti. Oh yes, it would be glorious if you could take some pictures of yourself and send me the negatives well packed in envelopes of black paper (and laid into your letter) and I could easily develop them of course. How wonderful that would be, I need them really badly. You know it is easy to get a little instrument to put on your camera so that it can take a snapshot (or even a time exposure) of yourself. Let me have you in different positions, the whole of you and every part of your beautiful body. How really wonderful that would be, and you know I could not get too much of you. As you like to have those of me I send you here two more which I have found, that may also be of "some interest."

I long for you so much, my darling, oh yes fancy, if we could only sleep together, as you say, ...yes indeed what a resurrection, how we would rise with new energy, and our work would be like a delightful play. Good night, my girl, I can write no more tonight, but I will dream about you, your lovely soul and "your hot violent body."

Fridtjof

July 12th, 1929

I may probably not be able to write before I have reached my quiet place in the mountains and it may therefore last some days. My daughter & wife came back last night and I am leaving the day after tomorrow, Sunday morning. Oh, I long to have a quiet hour or two or three to write to you. I kiss you and I press you madly.

Haukeli, Telemark,
Evening, July 18th, 1929

Brenda, my darling,

Now I am in the mountains and must send you a greeting. Here it is so beautiful, with the lake in front of my window, and the snow-mountains all round, and soon the moon will rise above the ridge on the other side, and life will be like a dream, and I long for you more than ever, and I think of you night and day, and especially in the night, and I wish you were here, we two together and far away from all people; oh, what a time we could have, what a wonderful time, and still more I would wish to go with you still further into the mountains to a lonely lake I know about, where there is plenty of splendid trout, and we two would live alone in a tent, and spend the day fishing trout and roaming about in the hills, and the nights in our sleeping bag, snug and warm, and oh, how wonderfully delightful to creep down into the bag with you and to feel your lovely naked body, and to hug you, and press you, with that wild nature round us, miles away from all people, and how we would love each other and how perfectly happy we would be.

The mail does not leave often here only three times a week. It leaves tomorrow and then I will send this. But even here letters arrive, disturbing my peace. Yesterday two long letters about the difficulties with the preparations for our polar expedition, and they want to send up hither our secretary from Berlin with his typewriting wife, to write letters for me concerning the expedition. But I will not have them, and see no use in it to disturb my holiday and rest, as long as no definite step could be taken for the arrangement of our station in Fairbanks, Alaska, which is the first thing to be done and which has to be done from Berlin where the experts are supposed to be. But it does not look very hopeful that they have not been able to do this yet, but rather prefer to go in for all other things which have to come next. Damn it, but why bother you with my troubles, I have had more than enough of it, have had to write a long letter about it this morning, and now enough about it.

Otherwise I have had some glorious days here, with sunshine and very hot, and feel a bit rested. My nice youngest daughter [Irmelin] is with me. (My wife [Sigrun] did not come now, she did not like to leave her garden. She may come a few weeks later.) She [Immi] paints in the morning while I am writing, and then we go fishing in the afternoon as a rule. But it is rather early for this yet, the fish have not begun to

97

take the fly readily; it will be better a little later, and we will therefore wait and rather work more now. But anyhow it is a nice life. It is a hotel on the tourist road across the mountains here where we are living. A few people, two English fishermen, are living in the hotel, and we see them daily at meals and have a chat about fishing and about nothing. Otherwise there are passing tourists staying for the night or having meals, and we are never bothered with them. There are sometimes a few of your countrymen (and women) too. I never spoke to them although I might have liked it for your sake.

I have a nice room with a wonderful view, and perfectly undisturbed; two beds, one for you, though you would prefer mine, I hope; not broad, but room enough if we lie close together in each others arms, and I do not think you would mind, would you?

I have been writing my book on Caucasus; but every minute I wish you were here as I want to read to you and to have your advice. Of course I write in Norwegian so I would have to translate. But oh, there are so many things I want to discuss with you and hear your opinion about both as to style and form and as to contents. It will not be much of a book though, and will not contain much, and nevertheless, I feel I have to write it, I do not know why. I have other things to write, which I think might be much more important and perhaps give more of my real self. Not that I think that to be so very important; but still it is perhaps the best I can give. Amongst other things I have some idea of writing a book giving my views on the various sides of life and its various problems. I would give it the form of a novel perhaps, and to some extent dialogs between a woman and a man. I have in fact once long ago written a first part of it; but I would have to entirely rewrite it, and now you would in many ways make an excellent model for the woman I want. But probably it will never come to anything, though there are things I should really like to say about different sides of life, and not least about love.

I have just now been writing an article about a prominent friend of mine for a work on the leading men of Norway, it is called "Våre Hövdinger" (i.e. "Our chieftains," or our leaders) [Våre Hövdinger : 70

livsskildringer med portretter/ ed: Halvdan Koht. 2 vol., Trondheim: Brun, 1929]. Your grandfather (Ole Gabriel Ueland) is amongst them, and also the grandfather of my children, (the father of my first wife, the great zoologist Michael Sars) and also my first wife's uncle (brother of her gifted mother) the poet Welhaven, and also my granduncle Count Herman Wedel-Jarlsberg. So you see there is much family in it. (I forgot that I am in it myself too.) The man I am writing about now is Axel Heiberg, who amongst many other things has supported me with my expeditions, and gave much money to the Fram expedition. He is mentioned in my book. He has given much to various things, science and art, but his chief merit is his splendid work for improving the woods of Norway, and for planting new forests and covering the land with wood. You might well need such a man in your country. But it is really very difficult to write those kinds of biographies, and I hate it, but had to do it in this case. I have nearly finished it now though, and it has not taken many hours, but how it is I do not know.

I wonder what you are doing, and whether you finished your story about architecture?

I wonder whether perhaps the mail tomorrow may bring a letter from you. How nice that would be. I long very much for it now. I shall also be very glad to hear how your dinner with Odd and Kari went off, and whether you had a nice time with them and liked their house and like them equally much, and whether you had any arguments with Odd, etc.

But it is midnight, everything so perfectly quiet as if we're alone in the wide world. It is dark out there, it has suddenly been clouded over and the moon does not show. The lake is like a mirror. I will have to go to bed. If only you were there! And I could take you in my arms, and I could feel your whole wonderful body and your still more wonderful soul, and you could have every bit of me, body and soul, and you could sleep with your head on my breast,... Oh, heaven! But I will go to bed and will dream that I have you with me, close and tight, and I love you above all words!
            Fridtjof

Address your letter to Lysaker as usual. They will reach me here if I am here still. Change the shape of your envelopes sometimes, though those you use are extremely good and business-like.

Friday evening, July 19th, 1929

Come, come, my dear girl, I long for you so sadly, I need you. It is so, I think, that a man is not complete without the woman. There is an empty space in my soul, a void, it craves you, come fill it. Come caress my soul with the dew of your sweet soul, come caress my body with the soothing touch of your lovely body. Come tell me that you love me, that you are mine, soul and body. I know it but still let me hear your dear voice saying it again and again. Tell me that life is still strong, and young, and beautiful, that there are still wonderful realms in the world that we shall conquer, you and I, come give me the wings of dreams and let us fly far, far into blue spaces. Come let me feel that life is not ebbing out, passing away slowly, and nothing worth having is achieved. Come let me see that the real things, the worthy things, the things worth doing, can still be done—those things, the chief ones, always waiting and beckoning in the future, but never reached—the real meaning of the life's work. Oh, your soothing voice in my ear, your dear hand stroking my neck and head and shoulder; your lovely body pressed closely against mine, the wonderful electric touch of your soft skin; yes how refreshingly beautiful you are: your lovely face, your head, every bit of your body. ...And we melt together into one heavenly dream, high above the earth and all its hideous trifles, far, far away from all cares, and troubles and worries dragging down, and there is nothing in existence but you and I. Oh, my darling, how wonderful it is. How refreshing, it is as if you had been here with me, and you have given me strength, and confidence, and buoyancy again; and life is bright and hopeful. Oh, my wonderful girl, what a power you have, and how I love you, and how grateful for all you give me. And now it is late, and I will go to bed, and will dream about you, till I fall asleep and hope the dream will continue.

Sunday evening, July 21ˢᵗ, 1929

Just a few lines before I go to bed. I long for you—have you ever heard it before? I feel uncertain and wonder whether perhaps it is not right of me to write such letters to you, it may possibly disturb your peace and your work, and that would be too bad. But what to do, I feel like it, and it gives me new life and you will forgive me, won't you? I am getting a little uneasy about your letters, I hope none have been lost, but it is much more than a week now since I got the last one of June 21ˢᵗ. and today came the third mail since I came here, and no letter, but plenty of other annoying ones. But nonsense, your letters do not go astray, there will come one with the next mail. Goodnight, my darling, I kiss you and press you and love you!!!

Friday, July 26ᵗʰ, 1929

A long time has passed. I have working hard with things that were pressing, and was waiting for a letter from you before I would send this. But two mails have come without any letter from you, and now I begin to become really uneasy. Has your letter gone astray, and come into the wrong hands? I cannot understand that it should be possible. But more than two weeks have passed without a letter; is it probable that you should not have written in that long time? Has something happened to you, or has really a letter been lost? I fear something may have happened, and therefore I am really nervous which is not my custom, but I have really anxiety for you, my dear, dear darling. Today a new mail will arrive. If there is still no letter, what shall I do? Shall I send this and disturb you with my stupid nervousness? Well, I think I better send it anyhow, though I cannot write much now, before I know that it is all right with you and your letters. My darling, I have been so depressed these days, because I have had much worry with the preparation for our expedition too, the people behave so foolishly I think, and have hitherto done so very little really efficient work, so it looks very doubtful the whole thing [will come off], as I see it. It is so annoying and more than that, [so much] time, and work, and thoughts spent on an undertaking which perhaps in the end comes

101

to nothing.

The life left is too precious for that and there are really much more important things to be done. But damn it! Never mind, when I think of you, I forget it for a while and there is at least something beautiful in life; and why worry; when only I get an explanation why no letters come, and I know that you are all right. I love you so, and isn't that happiness enough?

Fridtjof

P.S. Oh, my darling, I am so happy, the mail brought <u>two</u> wonderful letters from you written on July 5th and 7th, and everything is all right with you, and then with me too. But you see your last letter was finished on June 24th and then nothing in 12 days till July 5th. Now I understand, however, that was the time when no letters came from me when I was on the trip north. But I am happy now and relieved. There is no time for writing, as I must send this with the postman who will return in a short while. I will write later, as soon as I can. I may soon be disturbed though as probably in a few days I shall not be alone here in my room, and it may make difficulties, but never mind I will do what I can. Oh, I long for you more than I can say, my dear, dear Brenda, and I love you.

Fridtjof

Afternoon, July 30th, 1929

My darling, Brenda, I will write just a short letter, before I go out fishing to get a little exercise. I have been working hard these days, as I have to finish my book before I leave the mountains. I have just been writing about the brave Mohammedan mountain tribes in the Caucasus. They fought for victory or death. Victory meant liberty, death meant Paradise. And there were the Houris [beautiful, gazelle-eyed virgins awaiting Jihadi martyrs in Muslim paradise], smiling to them with black eyes like sparkling stars and arms like swan's necks, but not everybody will they embrace, only the brave ones. Fancy if you were the Houri waiting for me, how I would fight, and how I would seek the most exposed places, to get to you as soon as possible across the bridge Al-Sirat. And when I succeeded, and the right bullet found me, how you would receive me on the other side of the bridge, and we would never, never more be separated in all eternity. Why can one not believe in such a future? Fancy how much easier it would be to accept and give in to all the emptiness and banalities of present life. Really, I suppose, it makes the people happier; but indeed it would depend much upon whom one would have to meet in the other world? The Mohammedan could meet none of his women here, as they have no soul, you know, and therefore do not pass the bridge. But the Houris? Had they no souls either? What to do with them then? Their embrace is wonderful enough, I am sure, but one cannot go on embracing forever; and when there is no soul, only that beautiful body, what to do? One heard of no other enjoyments, only water-streams like diamonds rushing forth from milk-white marble to quench the thirst of the brave ones, on tall cypresses and shady plateaus in the cooling shadows of which they can rest. Not a very interesting existence really, except for those lovely bodies of Houris always ready to embrace probably. But the Christians are sitting on a white cloud blowing a trumpet and praising God forever; that seems much duller, and how tired poor God must be of all that praising; and what vain people it must have been to create such a Paradise. No, thank you, then I will rather have it, as it is, and I have at least the longing and the dream of you!! In the Christian Paradise there will be no sexual love of course, no embracing; one will only meet the Saints of this world, what an extremely dull company. But then the Holy Ghost? He had that love affair with the virgin, what about him? At all events, it does not seem tempting. By the way, I wonder how he came? Was it in the shape of a dove? That could not have given her much pleasure. Zeus came as a swan to Leda, that may have been better, or as a cloud to Io, and as the golden rain to Danaë, hardly very satisfactory; but as an ox to Europa that may have been well enough but very difficult, and hardly very attractive, and not beautiful. But it is strange indeed how a wild imagination has been at work in these things. It is strange too, how artists have loved to represent the charms of the embrace and sexual passion by painting Leda, and Io, and Danaë, with their swans, in all possible positions, and clouds and golden rain; but only not the real thing, which is the natural and beautiful one, when the male and the female melt together into one higher unity. It could be sublime, as I see it, but very difficult to do justice to it.

Oh, my darling, how happy I am, to have received your two letters at last, as I mentioned in my last letter sent Friday 27th. How strange that you say that my letter about my previous life and love-affairs should have any special merits, it was just an attempt to describe things as they happened and as I remember them, and to let you see a little of myself. Yes that clergyman's wife [Marie Holdt] was indeed a dear lovely woman, who made me much good, more than I can ever be thankful enough for, and our relation was so really good and beautiful, and I believe it was good and happy for her too, and she always loved me tenderly, and would do anything for me, more as her son than her lover, I believe; and she understood what a blessing she was for me. But that peasant-girl, isn't it strange that I always should repent afterwards that I did not embrace her? Perhaps after all, it may have done her more harm, perhaps, and roused her longings and craving still more? What you tell about your young cavalry captain seems very strange to me; that you should feel contempt for him afterwards, because he did not really touch you. I thought that after such a night, without getting the satisfaction you so much wanted, your passions would be so much roused, that you would long still more for having him fully in your arms, giving you all that you so badly needed. But perhaps you have not really loved him, and he has not been able to make you sufficiently passionate and it depends also, on what experience you had had, and whether you had had any man before; but when you thought: "Is this all it amounts to!" it seems as if you did not know yet, what it really was to have a man. But it is so different this from many girls, I believe, who like to play with love, and to have a man in their bed, and have him caress them in all possible ways, but do not allow him to get in too far, for fear of losing

104

their "virginity," which they wish to keep for the real one. But I do not have any experience, and cannot tell, really. Though perhaps—but about that another time, there will not be time now.

How nice to hear you tell about your visit to Odd and Kari, and that they and Signe and Marit spent another night with you, and that you like them so much. It makes me so happy. Yes they are really nice, and Signe too, I think; and they love you, that is also so nice!

I wonder where you are now? At Westport probably, or perhaps already gone to Minneapolis, for of course you miss your little Gaby. But I still address this letter to Stamford hoping that it will be duly forwarded to you, my darling.

As to that possibility of mixing me up into politics, which Odd spoke about: I do not know, I hate it, and do not think anything will come out of it; though many people wish it. I have always refused, but if it is my duty, I will have to do at least something perhaps; because the situation is really very serious, as I see it. But never mind, let us hope that my assistance is not needed.

As to the polar expedition, the preparations are advancing slowly, but what will come out of it I do not know yet. Anyhow a man is being sent to Alaska to arrange matters there. But now this letter is getting too long. I will finish and send it tomorrow. I thought I had so much to say to you, my dear, dear girl, and have said nothing, but I long for you more than any words can express.

Morning, July 31st, 1929

Now the mail is soon coming and leaving again so I must mail this. Today my wife is coming probably, and I will no more be alone, and there will be no peace for writing to you for a fortnight I am afraid, so do not expect much from me, I may try to send a few lines at least as soon as possible. I do hope you will understand though, and be patient. I went out last night fishing down the river, had a wonderful time and did not come back till nearly midnight. I love those nights between the lofty snow-mountains and with the river rushing along, and I wade into it, and the trout are rising, taking the fly, and the line runs out, and I play with them and take them in through the foaming waters. It is all so mysterious and beautiful, and you are in my thoughts and I only wish you could be there with me, how you would enjoy it. And then I would make up a fire, and we would spend the night there, together, wonderful, and I would have you in my arms, and when the day breaks we would fish again, and live the life of Savages.

I love you Brenda, my girl, I long for you passionately, and I am yours, every bit of me, body and soul.

Fridtjof

The mail just arrived, and heavens a wonderful letter from you of July 11th with the wonderful pictures which make me long more than ever, and feel happy, happy, and only to wish to take the lovely creature into my arms, and kiss you and press you wildly, and feel all of you, every bit of you, outside and inside, and feel your burning love. They are beautiful and how beautiful and perfect you are, face, head, heart, hips, belly, groin, loins, thighs, legs everything. The picture of you standing is glorious, and where you lie down supported on one hand so very lovely. Strange it is just the same pose as one I sent of me. I cannot answer your letter now, as the postman is leaving, but I thank you with all my heart, and kiss you and press you madly. Be careful to glue your envelope well together, it was half open, the cover had not stuck on one side. Never mind, nobody has seen it, and it had not been opened, as the other half was well fixed. But make it perfectly moist and _sit_ on it, then it sticks perfectly safely. Bless you, my darling!! Your envelope is excellent.

Wednesday afternoon, July 31st, 1929

My darling, Brenda,

The mail has left and I sent my letter, but now I wish to write a few lines more while I have a little peace, though I cannot send the letter before next mail on Friday. I look at your pictures, what a real blessing they are, it is almost as if I had you here. Oh, the lovely expression of your beautiful face in some of them where you are smiling at me, and that splendid body. Those arms, like swan's necks...

You say the only cure for your feeling of loneliness would be to have me around you and in you and over you, and you want to be in my arms under my "heavy hard forceful body." Oh, my darling, my darling, how sweet you are, and how I long to have that wonderful body under me, to feel it respond my caresses, to feel it tremble, and undulate in passion, to feel your arms and thighs embrace me wildly, to feel your burning fire and your tremulous flesh, yes it is all mine. You say that you think "love, the embrace, with its extraordinary feeling of safety, is just this longing back to the womb again." Oh, my darling, I am longing to...feel that we are one. Yes how wonderful it is, what perfect happiness!!

I am reading your dear letter over and over again, and [it] fills me with joy, and how very interesting it is. There are so many things I wanted to answer and speak about, but too little time for it now: What you say about love and all the various people, the Bohemians and the elegantly dressed snobs, and what you say about yourself "even as a virgin of twenty four without a glimmer of a sexual thought in any conscious brain." I should like to hear much more about that, and about your early views of love, etc., and what you would care to tell me about your experiences. But if you will rather not, never mind.

How very glad I am that you are getting on so well with your work. That relieves my conscience very much, then I have not disturbed your ability to write, and not disturbed your energy. How happy it makes me. It is really the same with me, I feel really unusually fit for work, although I always wish to write to you. What you say about Christ and Nietzsche, and the Ego and altruism is most interesting, and I quite agree with you, I think, and that "most of the time they were talking about the same thing." But about that another time, it would be too long now. You speak about attitude of men towards women. I think one reason why young men often disappoint young women and behave foolishly and make a poor impression, is that the men often think the women to be such ethereal beings, for whom love is something celestial, above all earthly and physical feelings. While in reality perhaps the young women are often quite as physical and earthly in their feelings as the idealistic, dreaming young men, who often associate physical feelings with the bad women.

You say: "Oh believe me—I would be just <u>perfect</u> for you." There is no doubt about it, my dear, dear girl, you would be perfect indeed and you are!!! With you around me, I would mind nothing; worries and people, or anything could not reach me or do me any harm then. Oh, my darling, I long for you, and how hard it is, that I cannot come to you at once, and how complicated and badly arranged this short life is! Yes I need, as you say, "safety, love, appreciation, viz. yourself; your arms around my neck, your hands so tenderly feeling me, my face, my breast, my loins." Bless you for everything you say, and for the comfort and happiness you give, my darling, my mistress, my love.

Your lonely "Viking" Fridtjof

Lysaker
Tuesday evening, August 27th, 1929

My dear Brenda, my darling,

Now I have been very bad to you, I have not written for a very long time, more than a week, nay ten days I think it is, and the last time I could not write anything either. I have worked like a madman day and night since I came back, to rewrite an important chapter of my book [*Through the Caucasus to the Volga* (1929)] and get it ready before I leave for Geneva. It contained many mistakes as it was, and now I have got new material. It is one, or rather two chapters about the fight of the tribes in Caucasus, Daghestan, for their liberty, and about Shamyl their great leader, and Hadji Mourád, the splendid leader of raids, who both interest me much as human types. Now today the chapters are rewritten, and just today I got your letter of the 9th in which you tell about your feelings towards Tomola, and that you and Anne two days later go to Minneapolis, and also that you have finished your article about the French gardener. I should like to read it. Oh, my dear, dear girl, how your letter makes me long for you, desperately and more even than I always do! I understand too, I believe, that you really need me, that I could do you much good if only I could be with you. I am afraid there is too much celibacy! You say that I am your man, your beloved, your complement (bless you!)...

...Oh, my darling, my darling how wonderful! And how I love you, and how I long for you, and I think it would be so good for you. When you made Tomola make love to you, I think it must to a great extent have been on account of your celibacy, you needed some sexual gratification, your nature demanded her right; but I wonder whether that gratification is sufficient? Whether you do not need something more, which only the male can give you? I think, however, that some celibacy is good and stimulating to a certain extent. The presence of sexual potency no doubt gives initiative, strengthens your imagination, and your productivity on the whole. Married people who sleep together every night lose certainly in mental vigour and get more sluggish, as you say. But accumulation of too much sexual potency, may also be disturbing and make you restless and nervous, and may disturb your ability to work. But perhaps that is still more the case with men than with women.

It is going better with the preparations for the polar expedition now, and everything looks more hopeful, though it means a great deal of work for me. I am afraid in about four days I shall have to leave for the Assembly of the League [of Nations] in Geneva. I hate it. This is my tenth year. I have certainly done my duty. I earnestly hope it will be my last. I shall probably be there towards four weeks, but address your letters here nevertheless. I have to finish now alas, and have said so very little of all the things I have to say. I shall write again as soon as I can, but it may be a little difficult to find the necessary quiet time for it, as I will not be alone on the journey unfortunately. I do hope you found Gaby all right, and that you are having a nice time in Minneapolis. How very nice of you to wish Odd and Kari to take your house, I wish they could, but perhaps it would be too far for him to go. I do not know what he is going to do, I believe he thinks he has had enough of planning cities now, and wishes to do something different. How I wish I could be in Minneapolis with you, what a wonderful time we could have. I love you my dear darling, my mistress, my every thing, and wish I were in your arms. Goodbye and do not forget your lonely Viking.

    Fridtjof

Saturday, September 7th, 1929

Brenda, my dear girl, my darling,

Here I am in Geneva, nearly for a week now, and have not yet written a line to you. – it has not been possible; but now I must try, though I am surrounded by people. Oh how I long only just to be alone and be able to write and talk with you quietly. I have just two wonderful letters from you (your first letters from Minneapolis) in which you tell your love stories and sexual experiences. I cannot say how thankful I am, and how very, very good you are to let me know so much about you, and let me look into your most intimate thoughts. – and how it proves what absolute confidence you have in me and how you trust me. But you see it is just the same with me, and I do wish to tell you anything, and not to hide a bit of my most intimate self. After all, that is perhaps the proof of real love. When I read your lovely letters, read about your experiences, and your lack of real sexual love, how it makes me long for you, to be in that bed with you (instead of the other one) to make you perfectly mad with passion, and to feel your wild embrace, and make you reach orgasm over and over again, penetrate you, melt together, forget the world, the universe, just you and I, and our passionate love for each other. Oh yes what a night we would have had, why, why did we not meet many years ago? What a time we could have had, and how different life might have been.

    Your letters make me see still clearer, how different in a way, the sexual feelings and longings of man and woman really are, they seem to be so much more complicated and mixed with other feelings with you. For a man, when his sexual feelings are roused, it simply, in most cases, becomes a question of sexual gratification. He must have satisfaction, and in the natural way. And for many selfish, rough, and brutal men this is the chief thing or perhaps even the only thing they care for. If they are strong with sexual vitality, one embrace may not be sufficient, they may need several in one night; but in that case they look upon their partner not merely as the means for gratifying their sexual craving, perhaps, but they have probably also some softer or gentler feelings for her.

But it is very interesting what you tell about your lover, whom you had in your bed, when you still kept your virginity. And you tried to help him as well as you could with your hand, but could not satisfy him, how touching and good you were. But he of course needed the whole of you to get gratification, it was not sufficient to feel your caressing hand, and to press his body against yours, he needed to be between your thighs, to penetrate into you, to be in your womb, to feel your love flesh round his swelling organ, to sink into you.

But it seems to me so strange that you could avoid feeling in the same way... The explanation must have been, that although you were curious and liked to get new experiences with a naked man and his sexual organs & body; you did not really care for him, at least not sufficiently to allow him to get too much of you. But if it had been me, even at that time, I wonder if it would have. ...You would be able to give yourself away entirely, to get perfectly lost, and enjoy it in all its glory. And you would get a feeling of obtaining real sexual gratification, ...and you would not get tired [but], would think it equally wonderful and delicious each time. And so it would go on the whole night, with a little sleep in between, after each embrace perhaps. But then you would awaken equally fresh and equally ready for a new embrace. How many you could take in one night? It would probably only depend on how many I could give you. You are so wonderfully healthy, and strong and vigorous, that there would hardly be any limit to your vitality. I believe that after say seven or eight embraces, you would not be tired, but quite ready to go on again, and would like to try it in all forms and variations, in order to experience as much and as many sides of me as you possibly could. At that time I suppose I could also have given you a great deal.
— — —

Well so I believe it might have been, and so I think it ought to have been, and I believe you would not have loved me less after such a

111

first night, and would not feel that now you had had enough of me, but would long for me again. But perhaps that is my vanity? And you may think I am boasting; but that is really not my intention and not my wish. My belief is, however, that such an experience would have been natural and sound for both of us. I am afraid that the experiences you had with the men, you did not care sufficiently for, and who could not truly rouse your love and your sexual passion, as would have been natural, was not fortunate for you, as it made you look upon sexual relations on the whole in a manner which was not natural, and therefore not wholesome, and it never gave you the wonderful satisfaction which you really needed.

There are so many more things I wanted to write about and tell you in this connection; but there will not be time for it now, as I must soon close and send this, in order that you may at least hear something from me. But my dear darling, do not for a moment think that because you write about your sexual life and your sexual feelings, it should make me think that those things fill your life and your thoughts to any unreasonable extent. Far from it. I think I understand you too well, and know perfectly what it means; But on the other side it is naturally a rather important side of our lives both yours and mine; that cannot be helped fortunately; it would be very regrettable if it were not so, and we would be very defective.

It's very strange that today I have just been with Emil Ludwig and his wife. My wife and I took them out for lunch at some restaurant in the country, and I was thinking of you all the time, and all you have written about him and about his book, [titled simply] *Napoleon*, which he has just sent me. But here I must stop. I love you, darling, and long for you more than I can say, I wish I could be in your arms, and let you really feel how much I love you, if ever that was possible.

Fridtjof

❖ Between the writing of the above letter, on Sept. 7, and the following letter, dated Nov. 20, the New York Stock Exchange crashed on Oct. 29 and thus began the worldwide Great Depression.

Brenda, my darling,

I must try to write a few lines before I go to bed; just to tell you what you have never heard before, that you are in my thoughts always, and that I long for you very, very much, and wish I were there with you, and that I could look into those wonderfully bright eyes, your lovely face, feel your dear arms round me – I wrote to you in the woods, I hope you have got the letter safely; but it was very hot, I am afraid. Was it too hot perhaps? And did it disturb you too much? Well, it is not wise perhaps, to write in that way, and I ought to improve, I dare say; but it is so difficult, when one longs so much, and you will forgive me, won't you?

I am back from the woods now, already some days, and am again sitting here in my tower. We had very rough weather, and here it was still worse while I was away, blowing a hurricane which has done much damage along the fjord, destroyed keys and bath-houses, and has entirely ruined a house I had down at the shore for boats etc., carried it away onto the land and crushed it to pieces. But never mind, it was not of much use any longer, and I can do very well without it. Otherwise, I have not much to tell about myself. After having finished my book I am working with different things, but have not settled down to any real new work yet, as there are so many different things to take care of. As to the polar expedition there is no news about the insurance yet, and whether it can be arranged, and I am waiting in uncertainty what to do. I cannot take any other steps of importance before this very important question is settled; but on the other hand time is passing, and it is getting late now for various preparations which have to be done. The whole thing is most unpleasant. But better not think of it just now.

I wonder what you are doing now, and long much for a letter, I expect from Stamford. You know, I suppose, that Odd and Kari have moved to East Orange in New Jersey now, and are very happy there, think it is a great improvement from Brooklyn, especially as Odd doesn't need to use the subway any longer though he has a longer way to his office, it takes him three quarters of an hour, about as much as from Stamford I suppose. I wonder whether you have seen them? But that may perhaps be difficult now? As they live on the opposite side of New York. How very sad! I hope you may arrange to see them somehow though.

But it is late and I ought to go to bed. I wish you were there, how wonderful that would be. Fancy if you were waiting for me in bed just now, and I came in to you, oh, my darling! How I long for you, my dear, dear girl. Goodnight.

Evening, Nov. 28th, 1929

Now a whole week has passed, and I have not been able to write. How very strange it was, when I came down in my bedroom after having written the above, there was a letter from you waiting for me. How happy it made me, dear darling, it was the first short letter from Stamford, oh yes, what consolation it always is to hear from you, and how I long for you, darling. In that letter you say that you have written to Kari and Odd in Orange in N. Jersey, so you know and that is a comfort too. Since then I have been very busy, and yesterday here was the wedding of my youngest daughter, Irmelin, to the Norwegian painter Axel Revold. No church-ceremony as she is a heathen but a nice luncheon party with 32 persons lasting till nearly midnight, while the couple left with the train for Egypt at 6 p.m. She is so very nice, and I love her dearly. She was the last one to leave the nest, and now the house feels very empty.

But then I have got a new letter from you written the 13th, and that is a great consolation, though I am sorry that you have got a letter from me making you think that I am so very depressed and "empty." Yes I was, but don't worry darling, it never lasts so very long with me, a few days rest in the woods and I am alright again. And tomorrow morning I am going away shooting again, and will probably not return for a week or more, and that will do wonders I know. But thus I cannot write much (now) as I must mail this myself tomorrow morning before I leave. How very sweet you are saying that I must

114

not worry about writing to you, as you will understand perfectly. Yes I know you will, and you are my dear good Brenda and my girl, whom I love more than I can ever tell you.

You write about your articles, and your many drafts. Yes I am convinced that your first draft is really all right; but you have it obviously in the same way as I have it. You think your products are never good enough, or at least never so good as you think you could make them, and after all that is perhaps the right ambition, but takes too much time probably.

What you say about Sigrid Undset's book [*Kristin Lavransdatter,* for which she won the Nobel Prize in literature in 1928] is splendid. I have read the two first volumes, but not the third. Then I had enough. There is too much religion, and as you say it is just fear, atonement, placation, I believe most religion is, either fear or hope for a reward. And there is no great motive in her persons, only sex and fear, and what you say about her maternal sensuality is very good indeed. Yes certainly the one sensuality is no nobler than the other. But more about this next time. I love you with my whole sensual body and my whole soul whether it is noble or not. Goodnight my darling my wonderful girl.

Fridtjof

December 14th, 1929

My darling Brenda,

Again it is a long time passed since I wrote, and I discover that I ought to hurry up if I shall reach you with a Christmas greeting in time. I am afraid I am already too late. I have been longing for a letter from you, it is some time since the last one now; but I know one will come very soon. Oh, my dear, dear girl how I long for you. So many, many things I wished to say, so many things to talk about, just to dive into your dear soul with all my thoughts, find rest and kindred thoughts, intermingle, just be ourselves and nothing else, far far, far away from this restless, empty, worrying, tiresome, disgusting life, which I really loath, and still have to go through and try to make the best of, and it gives no peace, always more than one can overcome. But I won't think of it now. What a wonderful blessing it would be, to be with you, dear Brenda, to hear your voice, to sink into your bright wonderful eyes, to talk to you about everything that is nice and beautiful, and loveable and to forget everything that is tiresome and ugly. I have your dear photographs here before me, and long to be with you more than I can say. Oh that beautiful head, and that lovely body, and those limbs!! I remember an oriental description of, "the most beautiful girl of the earth's globe." "Her bosom fetters everyone who sees it, thus its creator be praised – and from it two soft round arms issue. In front two breasts protrude like two hills of ivory and eclipse the splendors of the sun and the moon. She has thighs like two columns of the stuff of pearls, a waist softer than cream!" About another, the most beautiful of ten maids, is it said that "her naked beauty eclipsed the splendor of the moon; her thighs were full and tight like two columns of marble, or cushions stuffed tightly with ostrich feathers, her navel like a shrine of ivory; her bosom like diamonds; her neck like a silver ingot." Or, "her stature was like a Lance, her buttocks round, her hips slim so that they could cure the sick and satisfy the cravings of the glow of love." Oh, my darling, how wonderful it would be to feel that lovely body close to mine, to feel those arms round me, to rest between those beautiful thighs, on that belly, "like the full moon between black clouds." And those breasts, feel your dear hands caressing me, and then to sink into you and be dissolved and melt into one with you. You are my dear, dear girl, whom I love more than any words can express, and I long so desperately for you. And I know well enough that you long for me too.

But I must send this, in order that you may have at least some greeting from me for Christmas. I cannot possibly find words for what I would like to say but everything that is beautiful and wonderful I wish you, and all my best and nicest thoughts will go out to you my darling Brenda. And there is nothing worth having in me which is not yours.

Your Viking Fridtjof

My book is out now [*Through the Caucasus to the Volga* (1929)], and I am going to send you a copy, though you cannot read it. But never mind it does not contain much of value. Otherwise there is not much to tell about my life here, it is chiefly work and I had some days in the woods chiefly with pouring rain. The house is rather empty after Immi's wedding and departure for Egypt with her husband. Bless you!

January 20th, 1930

My darling Brenda,

Now it is very, very long since I wrote to you, but I have been waiting, waiting for a letter from you. Thought I would wait another day, and then another, to see if a letter should not come before I wrote, and thus time passed. Couldn't understand what had happened, was afraid there was something wrong, the worst was the thought that you were ill; that frightened me, but what could I do? I felt helpless, I couldn't write, for if so you may not be able to read my letters. — — But never mind now, I have three letters from you arrived almost at the same time, the two on the same day, and the first one only a few days before, and now I am happy again. You are a darling and I thank you that there was nothing wrong with you. I cannot write now, but will write very soon, there is no quiet time for it yet, so I have to wait. But your letters have made me so happy, and I long for you more than I can say, my dear darling and sweet girl. Yes let me have some new pictures of you, that would be very, very nice, and you know that I like them best in the costume of nature. Oh, how I wish I could draw you; I think I would draw you as the goddess of the woods, perhaps I could use a photo, especially if you could send me the negative, and I could enlarge it. But that is just a fancy, and never mind it may be very inconvenient, and may perhaps also be risky to send?

What you say about your book, which you wish to write, is highly interesting. I am sure you would write an excellent book, and wish you will get the time and opportunity to do it. I think your idea is splendid, and in fact a book of that kind would certainly be much more valuable than an ordinary fiction novel. I wish I could be there and help you, if I only could be of some use. There are things I wished to write too, and would need you badly to give advice, and to criticize. How wonderful that would be. Fancy this is actually the first letter I write to you in the new year. I send you all good wishes for it, and do hope we may meet soon, it seems a whole lifetime since we parted, and this life is really absurd. There is not much to tell about myself. Nothing of importance has happened, and I am working as usual. I should try to finish a great scientific memoir now on the oceanography and currents of the Arctic Sea, which my friend Professor Helland-Hansen and I are doing together; but he lives in Bergen, and does not come here often enough, so it takes time to finish it.

But here I have to stop. Do write soon, I long for your next letter, and I love you more than any words can express and wish that I could be with you in your nice quiet home and be your boy and your Viking,
        Fridtjof

❋ Nansen went up to a mountain hut at Geilo, on the Oslo-Bergen railway, for a reunion in the snow with two old skiing friends. One was Wilhelm Morgenstierne, a diplomat whom he had first met on his food mission to Washington in 1917-18. The other was Professor Jac. S. Worm-Muller, whose acquaintance he had first made in a sleeping car on a railway journey in Norway in 1914. They noticed that Nansen was not his usual self, so they kept to the easy runs. Morgenstierne had the 'flu. But after a few days Worm-Muller and Nansen returned to Oslo, blithe as usual. The evening of their arrival, Nansen talked to a military society on the different gliding properties of wood on snow. It turned out to be his last public lecture. Soon after, Nansen went down with 'flu himself, caught no doubt from Morgenstierne. He had had a heart attack while out hunting in 1928, and there had been other incidents since. But he had continued to press on with his work. —RH, *Nansen: The Explorer as Hero.*

February 28th, 1930

Brenda, my darling,

I am so sorry that such a long time has passed since you heard from me. You know that it is not because I do not wish to write, and you know that you are always in my thoughts whatever I am doing. But there has been so much disturbance lately, and I have been perfectly unfit for writing, and so I am still. I cannot say exactly what is the matter with me, but my brain seems so empty and will not work, and I miss you sadly, and still I cannot write a letter. Oh, if only you were here with me, it would be all right at once. I must send you a few lines though to let you know that I am still alive, and long for you more than words can express, and hope soon to hear from you again, perhaps that will rouse my sleeping brain again.

I have nothing of interest to tell you about myself, I have been to the mountains, skiing, hoping that it would help a little, but it was only for some days and not long enough. In March I am going for a few days to London where I shall deliver an address to the Royal Meteorological and the Royal Aeronautical Societies (in a joint meeting) on Polar Exploration on March 14th. I will only be there for three or four days, and then return home again. I do not like it much, as the future possibilities of realizing our plans seem still somewhat doubtful.

I am so glad that you liked my little drawing with the New Year greeting [see page vi]. Of course I thought of you when I drew it, I only wished I could have had you as a model. Then perhaps I could have done something really nicer. Having been unfit for brain work lately, I have made several drawings to rest my brain. I will send you some of the results.

I just had a letter from Odd, to tell me that now they have definitely decided to go back to Norway. He has been in great doubts, whether he ought to wait perhaps another year, and I was uncertain what advice I ought to give him. There are probably possibilities for him here now, but on the other side I am afraid that the economic future in Norway is still somewhat uncertain. It depends much on the political election in the fall this year. My regret when he leaves America will be that this link connecting me with you will be broken. What a pity. Oh what an eternity it really is since I saw you, and how I miss you, and how much I need you I cannot tell you, and I do believe that you need me too, though you may find plenty of others over there. But do not forget me, please!

I hope that soon I will be able to write you a real, nice letter, and

that you will have patience with me, for you know I love you my dear
girl and darling, and I long for a letter from you soon.

Your Viking Fridtjof

❋ He was now found to have phlebitis, a blood clot in one lung, and his heart was
beginning to fail. He was ordered to bed. Odd and his wife were called home from
America. King Haakon, who had kept his friendship with Nansen down through the
years, visited his sickbed. Nansen refused to rest, continuing to write letters and plan
new books. —RH, *Nansen: The Explorer as Hero.*

March 7th, 1930

Dear Brenda, my darling,

I am more sorry than I can say. I am tied to my bed for weeks and
cannot write to you. I have suddenly quite unexpectedly and without
any reason I know of got an attack of phlebitis in one leg, which is badly
swollen, and have had to keep in bed without moving. The doctor says
it is all right if only I do not move, but that is dangerous. How long I
shall have to lie here I do not know, but it may take some weeks yet.
I cannot write to you here, but will write as soon as I get up again. I
am so troubled about it; as you cannot understand of course only I do
not write; but you will understand now, when you get this, and then I
will probably be much better, probably out of my bed again. I have not
heard from you for some time now, but trust you are well and busy, and
soon a letter will come.

A thousand greetings. I wish you could be here, my dear dear girl.
Fridtjof

April 2nd, 1930

Brenda my darling,

I am so sorry. I am still lying here and cannot really write but will try
to send you a few lines. Have been in bed for more than a month now
and may have to remain there for three or four weeks more, so you
must not expect any letter from me for some time yet. After I sent you
a few lines I had a bad time: suddenly got a blood clot in one lung, and

it was a little serious. But I am all right now but must keep perfectly quiet on my back, and cannot do any work. It needs patience. How I wish you could have been here.

I got your letter where you mention your new l.a. (love affair). So very, very nice of you to tell me all about it, and you know I understand perfectly. You certainly need it, you cannot live so lonely. Oh, how sad that there is such a distance between us and that I do not know when we can meet. I also got your short letter with the film. I am so glad to have it. I wish I could do something really nice out of it. I think I could, if only I get the opportunity.

But now I cannot write more. Goodbye my darling, keep well and do not forget me. I love you and am your Viking.

Fridtjof

❧ This was Nansen's last letter to Brenda. His heart stopped beating on May 13, 1930.

[FROM NANSEN'S DAUGHTER-IN-LAW KARI,
WIFE OF NANSEN'S SON ODD, EIGHT YEARS LATER]

Polhøgda, June 2nd, 1938

Dear Brenda!

How lovely it was to have a letter from you. Thank you ever so much. Believe it or not, but <u>exactly</u> the day before I got your letter I was thinking so much of you and wish I could come in connection with you. But "Brenda Ueland, U.S.A."—I was afraid would not be enough!

I am sure I will make you happy by sending you this letter from F.N. I found it here by his papers just after his death, but I could not send it without your address. And for 8 years I have been still hoping you would give me a "sign" sometime.

I have always understood that you were in love with each other—and here at home some lovely pictures were found too—but we put them to fire because we were afraid some people could find them, who would not understand. I love you because I feel so well that you

121

had the right feelings about him—and he talked always about you to me—because we met each other over there.

We are still living at Lysaker—in the big old house of Nansen—but we are not the owner of the house. That belongs to the Videnskaps Selskabet. They don't know how to use it so we will stay here anyhow for a couple of years, I believe.

How wonderfully nice it would be if you could come and stay here for a time. I hope it is not hopeless for you to come over some day. Take Gaby with you! Is she really 16 years old? A nice lady. That must be just like having a good girl friend. I am sure she is a beauty.

I (or we) have 3 children. Marit is 9 ½. And Eigil is very much like F.N.—7 years, blue eyes and feisty and very much like Odd inside (and Odd is terribly like his father in everything!). And Siri is 5 years old—always laughing and thinks life is just wonderful. Of course it is wonderful too—but sometimes very hard and difficult to understand. But why should it be easy? (I have not spoken nor been writing English for years so I am afraid you will take lots of time to get through this letter. Next time I will try to do it better—but I have 100 thoughts in my brain that I should speak about to you and it is difficult even in Norwegian.)

Signe is secretary to a professor in the dental school and he is a big man who fixes all our difficulties with the foreigners in connection with <u>whales</u> (the big animals in the Southern Sea). Do you understand? She was near by getting married some years ago. But she came on other thoughts and by now she is free as a bird. She is so nice and lovely and I guess happy without a special husband and family. She is living together with my mother (who is the most lovely creature in the world), and my youngest brother, who I am sure you would fall in love with.

Odd has very, very much to do—and besides his architectural work. He has started a new "Nansen Aid" here in Norway to help the refugees from Osterreich [Germany] and other countries who have no place to stay or work; especially Jews, - but all nations of course – but the Jews have a terrible time out in Europe just now. This Nansen

Aid takes very much of his time too and he works much too much, and is sometimes very nervous and tired. He was in America two years ago and he would have loved to see you. But perhaps sometime we will have a chance to come over again. And then!

I am just finishing: "Gone with the Wind," a very interesting book. It is very entertaining. She must be a good author. Apropos books—I am waiting on "If You Want to Write," and I am so happy you will send it to me.

It is a wonderful time here just now—all flowers out, and birds singing, and children playing. It starts to be summer and that is the nicest time in Norway. I am going to the seashore for summer vacation – but not until the 10th of July. Before that I hope to get a new letter from you and maybe you can come this summer and go with me to the seashore.

Thousands of thoughts and love from Odd to you Brenda
– and from your friend,
Kari

A Sampling of
Brenda Ueland's Writings

*

"While you are alive be alive"
—Brenda Ueland

✍ *On Fridtjof Nansen: A Love Story* ✍

IN 1928 MY FATHER went to Norway and wanted me to go; but I was too anxious about making a living. He wanted to take care of all that, but there was my old complex about not being an expense, a nuisance. Besides, free-lancing is not like a salaried job. The work you do this month may not be paid for, for six months or two years, or ever. So I was dogged by conscientiousness. And all the time living expenses, rent and so on, went right on ticking off hundreds of dollars, like a kind of restless gas meter.

So I would not go. But I saw father off on the boat and felt sorry about it, and sorrier later, because on the boat he got to know well Fridtjof Nansen, the Arctic explorer. He was the great man of Norway. As well as an explorer, he was a famous scientist, a zoologist and oceanographer; he had been ambassador to London during the critical period of disunion from Sweden in 1905; and as the representative of Norway to the League of Nations, it was he who had repatriated millions of prisoners of war.

That winter Nansen came to this country. I read it in the newspaper. He was planning, it said, to go with Eckener in the

Graf Zeppelin across the North Pole, and he had come to make arrangements with the United States Government, for mooring masts in Alaska.

I wrote him a note and asked for an interview. I did not really want the interview so much as to see him and talk to him. This was my hero-worship. I felt that he was really great. If I could just get near and see him and hear him talk a little. In answer, he wrote me that he must go west but after that, when he returned to New York in March, he would surely see me.

And then it turned out that in Minneapolis, where he had to go of course, because there were so many Norwegians there, he stayed at our house. Julie [Brenda's sister-in-law, Julie Ueland, married to Sigurd], wrote and described him to me, and this is what she said: He was sixty-seven years old (I later found that he was born on the same day as my mother), a tall man with the most beautiful physique, a broad chest and lifted head, who was reluctant to sit down and stood up lightly, dwarfing everybody, and moved around like a quick young man. He arrived in Minneapolis the day after a blizzard, and this—the bright snow with the sun on it and the sub-zero cold—delighted him, and Julie said that he could not stay in the house, though many people were pressing to see him, but kept going out to the kitchen and on the back porch to breathe the snow and the air. And finding some old skis in the barn, old-fashioned child's skis without harness, he went hastening over the surface of Lake Calhoun without an overcoat and in his broad-brimmed black hat, followed by five floundering little boys.

In March he was in New York again. He wrote me a note that he would see me. He was staying at Mr. Henry Goddard Leach's house in the East Seventies, he said, and that I should come there.

The moment I saw him I thought: "Yes, he looks just as he should." He had bright color, a big nose, a wide white mustache slanting down like a Viking's, a bald forehead and skull and under his perplexed, intent, slightly scowling brows, there were level searching blue eyes, full of passionate intelligence and search, and a kind of anxiety-of-life and sadness in them. But the chief thing about his eyes was this striving search, this questioning, questioning.

Now my father also was in New York just then, at Anne's house [Brenda's oldest sister, Anny Taylor], and so at once I said to Nansen: Would he not like to go over there? My sister was so nice, etc.

"First," he said, "let's have the interview."

We sat facing each other by the window and he told me about the proposed trip in the airship across the Pole: the purpose of it, to make oceanographical discoveries about wind currents and ocean currents and zoological things. And he told why the trip was not a difficult nor a dangerous one, how there was little wind at the Pole, and so on.

I listened with interest, though knowing that I would probably never write it, except in my diary. I said that I would like to see him again. Yes, he said, he would let me know, as soon as he got back from seeing President Hoover in Washington.

And a week later he telephoned me; the Leaches, he said, invited me to tea. When I went in town to their house Anne and Father and others were there. I did not talk to Nansen, except that he said, just as I was leaving: "How did you get along with your interview?"

"Oh, fine," I said. I invited him politely to the country to see me, if he could find time; he could see the water there and hear the buoys; my father would be there in Stamford for a day or two. And in the next few days he telephoned me once or twice to Stamford, and his voice sounded placatory and gentle, almost anxious and tender; a "please-like-me" kind of voice. Would I come to town and have dinner with him perhaps?

And here is my diary:

Then I go to see Nansen. I dread this, think it may be hard work conversationally; am tired and stuffy from having too many clothes on. Work up my will-to-endure-pain as hard as I can, in preparation. To my amazement, when he comes in the room, he grabs my hands with such cordiality, holding them, talks to me. And so it is on the train. (We went out

127

to Stamford for dinner.) He keeps talking, so rapidly and eagerly, intermittently pressing my hand and in a confiding friendly way, smoothing the fabric of my coat over my knee, just the way I would if talking eagerly to someone I am fond of, like Julie or Gertrude or Henrietta.

Says he had a strange feeling about me—because of my first letter to him. He felt he must see me. Why should that be? He doesn't know. Perhaps because I said I had a sister, who was very nice, and that sentence proved that I was. He said that at the first interview, when he put off going to the Taylor's house, where Father was, that he was pretending he wanted to give me an interview so as to be alone with me. Very, very strange. I have mixed feelings. I don't know whether it is that he is a man with a great deal of temperament for women, or whether it is myself personally. He tells me about his boy who died of brain tuberculosis and who said: "I have such extraordinarily interesting thoughts;" and then he would tell his father that now he must leave the room, because he was going to have one of his seizures, and they were terribly painful. Nansen says he has never spoken of that to anyone. And he tells how one day he came downstairs and his child was crying. A governess had punished him for eating some grapes that his father said he could have. Nansen comments on how children are not allowed to defend themselves. And he says, with a wince of feeling, how he has always wished this had never happened, how he should have turned out this disagreeable woman.

It is queer. We talk like this together. I speak and he listens so eagerly. "Yes, yes.... Do you think so?"

My diary ends here. But these are some of the things he told me. He had been a very vigorous wild strong boy, a skater and a skier, a sailor and a huntsman. His father wanted him to go into the army or navy, but this did not satisfy his intellectual cravings. Yet he could not bear city life, indoor life. (People in cities, he said with abhorrence, were like bugs running from box to box.) He decided to become a zoologist, for that would permit all kinds of exploring in the mountains and northern rims of Norway, and at sea too.

In 1888, when he was twenty-seven, he crossed Greenland, which had never been done before. He decided that all the failures of the past were due to this: they tried to cross from west to east, so that they could always retreat to their base. But he would try it from east to west. With no line of retreat, they would have to go on. And this was one of the greatest principles of his life. "Burn your boats and demolish your bridges behind you. Then one loses no time in looking behind, when there is quite enough to do in looking ahead; then there is no chance for you or your men but *forward*. You have to do or die."

A few years later when he was thirty, he went on his Arctic expedition in the *Fram* (it means "forward"). Nansen had found, in his zoological studies and by other evidence, that there was a continuous drift of ice across the North Pole. In this ship, built to stand great ice pressure, they pushed as far north as possible, became frozen in for three years, so that they would very slowly be carried by the ice, and drift across regions very near the Pole. At the nearest point, Nansen and one other man, Johansen, left the *Fram* with dogs and guns, and struggled toward the pole on foot. They got to a point about a hundred and twenty-five miles from it. Then the arctic winter caught them, and instead of the three months they were provisioned for, they had to live through fifteen months before they got out. Their dogs were eaten. They shot bear and walrus and for ten months tasted no other food.

But this adventure and escape were not just a happenstance. It was thought out with Nansen's extraordinary foresight so that they came through it all right.

"You may think it was hard," he had written in a little book called *Adventure*, a rectorial address at St. Andrew's University, "but I assure you it was a happy time, for we had the spring and the homecoming to look forward to. In these plans I had most of the competent authorities of the world against me. However, I had the advantage of living a great deal alone in my life and had thus acquired the habit of making up my mind without asking the opinions of others. Not that every man who stands alone is strong. For a strong man there is a great danger in obstinacy and foolhardiness. It takes a superior man to allow himself to be convinced."

Well, I find myself so anxious to tell what a remarkable man Nansen was, but all this you can read. You want to know what he said to me.

He talked about Ibsen. He could recite whole passages of "Brand" by heart and in English. He told about his children, his wife who had died. He talked about my grandfather, Ole Gabriel Ueland. He described his house in Oslo [Polhøgda] and the tower that he worked in. He told how he had become surly and lonely after his wife's death. He told about his work in the League of Nations, repatriating prisoners of war and how it was exhausting and he would like to give it up, but he could not be supplanted, for governments and prime ministers would not act for a lesser man. He admired me for not smoking or drinking. He said that the reduced food rations in Europe during the war had been hard on the children but had improved adult health.

Gaby [Brenda's daughter, born 1921], who was ready for bed, appeared at the top of the stairs to say that she would like to be told a story. He went upstairs at once. He told her about the time in the Arctic that the kayak with guns and supplies in it had slipped off the ice ledge and was being blown lightly out to sea. He had to take off his clothes and swim for it, in that freezing water. It was the only thing to do. He had to go very fast too, and Johansen stood on shore and looked on in agony. Nansen caught the boat, but the hardest thing of all was to get in it, because he was so frozen and weak. Gaby liked the story. But she thought they should not have shot walrus or bears. That made her indignant.

The next day, when he was gone, I had the strangest experience. I felt the usual mild relief one has when a guest is gone. "Now that's over," with a mental dusting of my hands. The house was quiet and the sun was shining and I could work again.

At one o'clock I went for my usual walk, far around to the other side of the Point, and before turning back I sat for a moment on the yellow sand in the sun. As suddenly, as if I had been hit by a bludgeon, I seemed to be in love with Nansen.

This is my diary, a few days later.

Friday, April 15th, 1929

I go to town, arrive 4:40, and go to the Leaches'. Nansen is there, but his son and daughter-in-law [Odd and Kari] cannot come. We go to dinner. I am alternately all admiration and misgivings. A Norwegian accent always seems so gentle, almost womanish, so harmless, when he looks like a Northman on a ship about to kill a thousand Saxons. He should have a helmet with two tall wings on it. But then his sudden smile, softness and gentleness, is attractive and warms one towards him. He speaks of women who paint (they are all about us in the restaurant); speaks conventionally about this. I argue the point. I say it is all right to try to be handsome, though I don't like to try to be alluring, soft. But I try to be handsome with all my might. He laughs and says, "It can't be hard." He also says, "How dark your eyes are," and I do not explain how much I prefer light eyes.

Then we go back to the Leaches'. He tells me how when he returned from Washington he went straight to Anne's house, made a fuss about missing Father, but how it was myself he wanted to see. But, he said, from Anne he finds out all about me. Says how he pressed my hand, and how I returned it too, just once, very faintly. I cannot quite remember this.

He says I must have his pictures. And he gives me his books, a few of them in paper covers, and he sits down to the desk to write in them and I have misgivings. Am I in love with him? No, it seems so queer, so mysterious, too unfamiliar.... But when I look at some rolled papers on his desk, he says I may look at them if I like, and they are his drawings. And I think how modest he is about these, and I am overcome at their excellence and wonder that his very large thick hands have done them. And then I have the strongest feeling that he is a great man and a Viking and sincere and tender and strong and full of self-understanding and self-criticism and full of appreciation and delicacy and will and mightiness and nobility.

Earlier in the evening he said he needs someone to talk to, and speaks of *Faust* (cannot remember what he said) and I speak against marriage. But he says one cannot be alone; there is always a feeling of incompleteness in a man. We speak then of children, or morality. He listens to me with respect.

I take the eleven-thirty train to Stamford. He comes down there with me. (He was leaving for Norway the next day.) And when he says goodbye to me and kisses my hand, I shall never forget his face and I know that he loves me, for there is the terrible look of the sense-of-eternity, or the sense-of-death in it. In the cab on the way to the train, he spoke one sentence of great sadness. "I wonder if I will ever again..."

For a year we wrote to each other every week, until his death. We had a plan that when he came the next spring to go in the airship across the Pole, I would go with him. He would arrange it.

I was so much in love with him that it was hard to keep from writing to him all the time. I could easily spend five rapt, vanishing hours on a single letter. And a letter from him was the light of my days, and I have never in my life felt just this way at any time. The most disconnected things would sing through me like music, just looking out on a spring morning toward the Sound, toward the poplar tree and the tangled ragged meadow of gorse. The words: "Whose name is writ in water" went across my mind, and such a strange and unconnected thought like that, but it struck me and sang through me and made gold harp wires of me. Those words and something vague about Keats would make tears of inexplicable rapture come into my eyes.

Of course when I think of my letters to him, I have my usual dislike for myself of yesterday, because they were so planned, so composed. I wrote them over and over, as though they were poems. That wish to be effective—I am always so afraid there is insincerity in it. Yet I did love him unutterably and there has never been anything like it.

And all the time, you understand, it was a sort of dream love affair, a literary one. We never really believed we would see each other. And yet I know my letters were comforting and exciting to him. I can tell that from his. And I am so glad they were.

April 25th, 1929.

You cannot possibly understand what your letter meant to me, it is as if a flood of strength suffuses my whole body and soul, and I feel that you are near. How very sweet of you to write so soon. I needed it badly, as I felt lonely. And what a letter! Just you, as I was sure you must be.... There is not a corner of my heart or soul which I do not wish you to look into— not because I think that there may not be so much which is ungraceful or offensive, but simply because it is all parts of my own self, and you have to know it. I have a feeling that I could talk to you about everything, as I have *never* before, and you would always understand.

...But you know nothing about me! It is equally strange that when I got your first letter, I already felt an inexplicable attraction towards you, and had a vague anticipation that I would like you very much, and that perhaps you would like me too. And after I had heard your father speak about you I decided that I had to meet you, and that we would understand each other, and had much in common.... And I had that letter with me and your second one too, on my journey west. And I read it again and regretted more and more, that I had not made a special effort and gone out of my way to meet you,

133

already during those first few days I had in New York. But anyhow, what a great thing it was that we met at last. But distinctly I remember you the first time, in that blue tight coat that suited you so well, trimmed with fur...

But we ought to be thankful for what we had, and I am, more than I can say. Yes and how good and dear you are and how beautiful. Though I miss you every moment, still how rich I am. You see recollection is the only Paradise from which we cannot be turned out...

How really absurd it is, so short is life, and still we cannot arrange it and these few flying years as we know would be great and wonderful.... Your letter—I never received any letter like it, never experienced such a revelation of personality that I could give myself to without reserve.

From my diary (May 16th, 1929) I find this is what I wrote to him in one letter:

1. About being in the public library and reading about him and feeling inferior to him.
2. His letter changes me from an egotist to an altruist.
3. About my asceticism, and how I never know whether to be a good-natured Negro or a stern Spartan.
4. About my faith: everything will come out all right.
5. How people's shame causes others to be scandalized. For example, Lord Byron; so wicked yet not ashamed and the world admires him.
6. How if we could only be together (*fused*) as he says, then I could have his blue eyes, legs, his nose, his brow like the infant Hercules, his skull like Socrates. He could have my black hair and brown skin.
7. How people who loved each other, the bond might be so strong that, paradoxically, there would be freedom. "In loving bondage, free," said Nietzsche. Like that.

134

On May 13th, 1930, he died. *The New York Times* said that when Norway had separated from Sweden in 1905, they asked him to be king, but he would not. The English *Athenaeum* said that he was "the greatest European" because he was a great scientist, a great explorer, a statesman and a humanitarian. He had also been skating and skiing champion of Norway as a young man, and was never beaten in either. As for me, I have thought of him every day since then. He thought that we were extinct after death. I childishly think I shall see him again.

✦ *Excerpted from Me, courtesy the Schubert Club, first published in 1939 by G.P. Putnam's Sons*

✺ Selections from Brenda Ueland's diaries ✺

BRENDA EDITED HER DIARIES in 1969, and again a decade later, before bequeathing them to the Minnesota Historical Society. The following entries are selected from among the few that remain. —EU

Thursday, July 18th, 1929

T. [Tomola] for dinner at Stamford Yacht Club. Hard as steel towards me; and I vary between being wounded and disdainful. But also, Tomola softens in flashes. I am afraid our bodies lead our intellect about by the nose, and we think it is our intellect telling us things, but it is our intellect simply finding reasons for what our bodies command us to do.

Good advice from Tomola. First, (she says) I am self-centered like Father, and perhaps Elsa [Brenda's second oldest sister]. This introspection [is] no good, or very little good. And I am variable. An even keel—that is the thing. And I agree. Perhaps, if all this maundering introspection were turned into action, instead of this tiresome experimenting with character, if I tried to accomplish definite things: 1.

Acrobatics, 2. Tennis, 3. Fiction writing, 4. French, 5. To learn something.

And I see in Tomola this hardness, (Nietzschean), its force and strength and steadiness. I wish I were that way. Perhaps the assumption that one is wicked, bad, hard, is really the correct one and so a person has a wonderful integrity and sincerity, an indifference to approval, etc., etc. And therefore the inevitable flashes of generosity are so honest and so deep, not adventitious. There is much in this. I guess my mistake is my everlasting expecting myself to be so damned perfect and noble and everlasting failure is the result and a permanent sense of guilt and a permanent sense of hypocrisy.

But no more of this character conjecture. I am now going to act, not meditate. Yes. No more introspection, but action. I shall not take these long indulgent walks thinking about myself; no wonder I avoid people—this is a flight, like that of so many people around me.

Friday, July 19th, 1929
...Want to smoke. Not more than an hour's sleep last night. Confusion. Gratitude. Yes, the assumption that I am a conscienceless liar, self-seeker, is quite right.

Saturday, July 20th, 1929
Carl is home today. We take a walk. I turn many handsprings. I do not think about myself, nor have these philosophical maunderings. A letter from Nansen. My confusion increases. Go down to the Beach Club. Swing. Craving, craving to smoke. And yet, if I do, is this not the unsteadiness that Tomola speaks of? Is this wish to smoke the result of my confusion, or is it because I no longer wish to be introspective and philosophical? Or is it because I have decided, in order to be more with people, more sociable rather than aloof, that I have to take upon myself some of the things that make

sociability easier? Or is it myself imitating Tomola? My horrible suggestibility? I don't know. But I am afraid I am going to smoke.

Saturday, September 6th, 1929

Cocktail party at Julie's [Brenda's sister-in-law Julie Ueland] and then we go and dance at the Boulevards of Paris, and I am dull, bored, sluggish and have very little fun, except in talking to...Phil Foley, who has been a brick-layer.... I decide it is the unwieldiness of a large group that makes them hard, how two or four might have come to that place and had a good time.

And then, sitting in a great circle, I say to Henny that what is oppressive is the feeling of captivity, that if I were truly independent and wanted to walk up and down the stairs I could not for the unseen clammy hands reaching out to me, the curiosity—Why? Where? Stay here? Yet, I say, is there any reason in the world why one should not get up and quietly and good naturedly and sweetly go upstairs and say briefly, with the greatest amiability in the world, "I am sleepy. I'm going to bed." There is none. It is just that we are not independent, free and upstanding. Herd animals, damn us anyway.

Monday, September 8th, 1929

Leaden sky and heavy rain.... As I start out to walk [I read the most recent] letter from Nansen and it is very ardent, but it does not interest me, but rather fills me with some ennui, disappointment I suppose, that there is no more definiteness of a turmoil than before, such as Julie has been jokingly suggesting [that Brenda marry Nansen]. Yes, I guess that is it. Really, what a lot of foolish speculation I have been indulging in.

Today I think that my reasonableness, "my sweet reasonableness," has made me a little namby-pamby and there has not been enough will and fire in it. This I must cultivate, a decent austerity and sternness with myself.

And I should cultivate definiteness in everything—in dressing, in thoughts, in writing notes, in my diary. I ought to write definitely what my plans are, what I wish to achieve, whether it be in taking notes on Matthew Arnold, reading certain books, drawing pictures or what. This vagueness is my chief fault.

Tuesday, September 10th, 1929

A blue, wet, clear, limpid day. I take a walk around [Lake] Harriet, and when I have gone for some time I think how it is my will, my effort, that has been lacking. Too reasonable I have been; no force. This thought fills me with it...how poor our reason is; our affective feelings are what make our so-called reason. I must read those two volumes of William James, psychology, and really learn a little about all this. I will.

...I have many qualms for my stinking unsociability. Really, instead of taking credit for our irritation at others—as though they were to blame and we were so superior—why do we not see the truth, which is our irritation at others is not their failing at all but our own, our lack of vitality, and other things: for if we were as we should be, as independent, high spirited, affectionate, generous as we should be, why no others could trouble us in the least. At dinner [I'm] on the verge of [making] a Prohibition argument, [against drinking alcohol]. Me against all. But I am disgusted at the fact that my emotions are involved, and am really near petulance. What an ass [I am]. I wish I could improve a little.

Wednesday, September 12th, 1929

A quiet day, the house empty, my enterprise returns. Work fairly hard, though I break my typewriter...it is interest that prevents fatigue.... Certainly, in conversation, boredom is what makes fatigue so frightful. If...you can only get interested, [you are] no longer tired. Perhaps this is a tip for writing. I must try to get interested in it and not make it a duty. That is why it is so much easier to work towards the end than the beginning. Yes.

Tuesday, October 22nd, 1929

Tomola and I talk almost all night. My letter that I thought such a marvel of honesty and justice and that I thought would please her so, has thrust her into blind rage and fury. It seems that any mention of my "remorse" does this. And what also causes rage is any "bunk," i.e. compliments, appreciation. Well this is interesting and I feel as usual like a hypocrite, a liar and a fool.

My new maid arrives today. And I think how Tomola and Tookie [Tomola's partner] and the others, unlike heterosexual people, seem so strange, tense, queer compared to others. Perhaps it is true they hate procreating humans and there is a great gulf between the two. Perhaps because there is no parental instinct, which is tolerant and forgiving and serene. Well I don't know. But then I observe that when I am hard, Tomola softens. But when I am soft, she hardens.

Wednesday, October 23rd, 1929

A raining, sodden, wild grey day. I meet Tomola at the ten o'clock train drawing to the station under a black, balmy, wet-but-rainless sky. Tomola comes in and talks with me. I feel so happy because this night there seems to be for the first time ever a lightness in our relations. She laughs so heartily and makes fun of me. She roars, and I roar back with equal hearty vehemence saying, "By God, I'll argue with you about that!" And then she stops and looks at me, suddenly the most charming, friendly, gay and affectionate smile. And so it goes. She says I like her better tough and how she has learned to cap a vile story by another worse one. I say imagine God being horrified at dirty stories.

Then Tomola speaks of our fighting and I say, "Why not fight? Why not turbulence and violent feelings?" Probably our trouble was only the prissy feeling that fighting was terrible, a disgrace, and so was jealousy. There is no disgrace in violent feelings if one is not righteous about it and does not interpret it to one's own splendid-ness but sees through it and understands it, whether it is egotism, appetite or what.

Today I must work on my Dressmaker's article for the *Saturday Evening Post*. Be industrious, more industrious than anyone in the world. Every half hour is precious. Industrious, bold, diamond-hard, honest, generous, independent. And I must make Gaby happier, happier than any child has ever been.

Saturday, October 26th, 1929

A sad windy day and depression begins about 11 o'clock. I walk (5 miles) at 2:00 pm and fight it off. Inferiority feeling. Loneliness. How strange these things are, this fear and longing to be loved and doubts about it. It must go back to meagerness within, low vitality and so an incapacity to love others.

But I walk dreamily in the wind.... My meditations this day, out of which I seem to draw consolation, are these: delight in pain, in combat. Sock for sock. Affectionate pugnacity. Al Smith and Bernard Shaw. I do not mean pain seeking, and enduring, like a martyr, but jovial have-effort-pain, enduring blows, all of them, with robust, good-natured willingness. Bloodied but unbowed. And laughing. How strange we are.

Sunday, October 27th, 1929

Again I am painfully aware of my cruelties. What to do about that? (1969: "Cruelties"—what were they? I don't think I have ever been cruel. I think it was this—to escape from emotional slavery to Tomola I had fallen in love with Nansen. Now— he in Norway—I felt the pain of separation for her barking,

140

passionate admiration. She had become self-protective, cautious, successfully antipathetic to me. I felt forlorn and so remorseful, as though I had actually been cruel to her. She was ruthlessly cruel to me in her domineering, threatening possessiveness. I really think this was so, now from this distance in time.)

Tuesday, November 27th 1929

Margaret Norris here. When the doorbell rings I say to her, "I wonder if someone is coming to foreclose the mortgage." But it is a kind, gentle, affectionate letter from Costain [Brenda's editor at the *Saturday Evening Post*] saying he likes the "Dressmaker" article. So I am full of high spirits. I get $850. Feel as though I would never worry again, so rich, solvent, free. Yes, now I must really get rich. I think really I may now be established as a successful person.

(The Depression begins—it is Dec. 20, 1929. We are not aware of it yet.)

The following abridged letter from Brenda to Nansen, which Brenda entered into her diary, is the only surviving letter from her to him that has been found:

Monday, February 24th, 1930

Darling Fridtjof,

I have been working very hard and this is not just the usual protest of one who has been soldiering, malingering, (which is usually so in my case), but I have sworn to write an article in two weeks, instead of taking the usual five or six...

Today I am kind of tired, not enough sleep and too much work. But it is a glorious day with thick yellow sun drowning the earth and it is as warm as May and so it has been for three or four days, so that I go walking without stockings or sleeves and have already a thin, mottled, jaundiced looking tan. I have

141

so much to tell you. I ought to tell you everything, but there is so much. That is the trouble with writing so infrequently, if one could only write every day, one could write many pages. But when it is put off there is too much to tell and so it only becomes a bleak resume. But now I will see what I can get said.

I feel quite sad because inevitably our vigorous interest in each other must wane a little, though this is only because of discouragement and because there is no certain possibility of seeing each other. But if only the definite possibility turned up, say I heard you were coming to this country, six months from now, why my feelings would be revived in all their fierceness. I wish you <u>were</u> coming...

There is a man in love with me now and I have experimented with a love affair again; a nice, nice honorable manly fellow whose wife is away in Florida and who does not love him at all though he is too simple and honest to be aware of this. She leaves him for six months every year and then he must live alone in a boarding house in Bridgeport and his company is failing and carrying down in its crash all his money. (His wife has money of her own.) So I have been very good to him, make him come down here for dinner, got him to fall in love with me. You once said that in your case, flirtations and so on were due to the explorer in you and this is true in my case also...Ah well, we are all complex...

Tuesday, May 13th, 1930

Nansen died today. Today I cannot take this in.

Wednesday, May 14th, 1930

Nansen is dead; today my feeling of loss comes in full onslaught. Once they wanted him to be King of Norway. And reading his letters I feel how little, how meagerly I wrote to him. Could have done so much more. It will be so I suppose when anybody we know dies. We have no idea what depths of

142

emotion there is in us; it is as though we had been counting on giving them thirty years of affection and suddenly there is no outlet for it and it is all pent up. Odd and Kari went a month ago. How stupid, dull of me not to have learned from them that it was serious. And my last letter to him was so loathsomely optimistic; but at least I must have said in it much that I...[undecipherable]...

Tuesday, May 20th, 1930

At 12:30 in this windy but sunny day I go for a long walk—go the whole length and then around my Nansen coast. How I feel the vacancy he has left...

On my walk I criticize myself for my weak, sociable tongue-wagging. Disgusting. And it has its effect, for this morning I do not tell everything. It has its effect in spite of myself, and without my jaw being grimly set. Thus the imagination-reason works and creates us. And I hereby will make myself unflinching, bold, truthful, strong, generous, and fiercely and relentlessly decisive in all things concerning self-control...

Friday, May 23rd,1930

I seem to be cross, a little, underneath. And yet full of energy. When we are so, one should not necessarily wrestle with one's disagreeable emotions, cannot suppress them very well. The thing is to do the most consummatingly generous act for those whom we resent; let the resentment inside remain untouched, like a snarling beast; but always the generous act. This makes the feeling vanish.

Sunday, May 25th, 1930

Reflections: I must get myself to work with more persistence and doggedness, as Margaret does. How much she accomplishes. I must do this. Get over my complex. I just try to solve the ethical dilemma of transparency versus silence.

143

Perhaps the only thing that makes telling seem so weak, is one's qualms afterwards; one can't stand by one's blabbing, but gets afraid of others' opinion. That may be part of it. And if one blabs so, one should also be willing to do it before the people involved. Well, I must work this out.

And then I think, coming home in the car, and say to Margaret how perhaps we should be fiery and strong enough not to get attached; all this love nonsense, all the thought expended on it and its aura of sentimentality. Ridiculous. And how when one becomes fixated, all the future is shut down—all the mysterious adventurous exploring future. That is as soon as you have that glorious feeling "I have fallen out of love" then one thinks of being in China, Tartary, the trans-Siberian railroad, seeing and learning all things. Yes.

Monday, May 26th, 1930

I cannot bear men who work indoors.... It was why I liked Nansen; sea captain and skier aspect of him, best of all.

After the movie we go to her (Avril's) house and talk. This breaking of rules makes me garrulous; or surprisingly, thought comes out in speech that I have not thought for months, years. But I must become ascetic again, and silent. That is best.

I think how all that I am has come from reflections when I walk; my strength lies in that. Otherwise I am commonplace. The happiest and most memorable and fruitful periods in my life have been those when I walk interminably, thinking, thinking.

Thursday, May 29th 1930

I walk home from the Ford repair shop, in this blue watery sunshine. I think about the problem of my garrulity, my loose-tongue. And I have these arguments against it: First it is self-indulgence because I am flattered at the interest of people in my gossip. Second, it is weakening to all my feeling and convictions and lets off all force and energy. Third, why should I subject my friends (whom I talk about) to the adverse, derisive, or misunderstanding opinion of a dozen others, since all opinions have their effect? No, I will not do it. It is pure self-indulgence.

Then, out of Plotinus, I read how eternity is now, there being no past nor future in it—the eternal now. So much of my weakness in willing etc. is because I think of myself always in terms of the future. I should have instantaneous strength, courage, decisive firmness.

❧ *From Brenda Ueland's diaries, Minnesota Historical Society, courtesy the Schubert Club*

๛ *The True, Little Known History of Women* ๛

ROBERT GRAVES, the poet and historian, says, "The most important history of all for me is the changing relationship between men and women down through the ages."

For thousands of years there has been a tragic situation—the domination of men and the degradation of women. We are so used to it we do not notice it. The situation has begun to change, but very little, and going back, I will show you why in a minute.

This was not always so. Now there is an underlying feeling that true equality is impossible because men and women are so different. We can never be like each other. But I disagree. We once were and we must again become noble equals.

Two things stand in the way of this: the age-old egotism of men, their anxious jealousy of women as equals, their touching infantilism, their dire need—all interwoven in their *amour-propre* to dominate women. The other thing that holds back the equality of women is our acceptance of our own feebleness, our physical weakness, our work to make a kind of virtue of it as a self-sacrificing sweetness, gentleness, and nobility. But this is wrong, too, as I will show.

Our weakness, smallness, and athletic ineptitude has come about because for four thousand years we have degenerated. Due to what? Male domination.

Fortunately women inherit from their fathers as well as their mothers. If all women were weak, cowardly, and flightily stupid it would not be so for more than one generation. But due to this imbalance, something regrettable has happened to us.

In fine wild animals—lions and lionesses, mares and stallions—there is no inequality. A mare can run as fast as a stallion. A lioness is about the same size as a lion and just as brave and capable.

Now go back three thousand years to Asia Minor, the first civilization that was somewhat stable. In those happy and far-off days women were deeply respected and loved by men and had a kind of wise command over things. This was evidenced by the greatest queen of all time perhaps, Semiramis of Assyria, a great, wise, and beneficent ruler. And she had another quality of women then—bravery, for she was also a great soldier. In fact that was what especially charmed her husband. She reigned for 42 years. And she realized, with the modern Einstein, that the only way to have a better world was to have better people and the design for her religious system was to achieve this. We know this from the Mystery Religions of Egypt, Greece, and Rome, all of which varied only in superficialities. When Semiramis died, after insuring that Babylon was the most magnificent city in the world, she was deified.

Now the goddesses of the Mysteries were all believed to have been originally extremely wise human beings and owed their deification to this fact. Ceres was said to have brought agriculture to mankind—which was one of those talented inventions of women. Cybele the Phrygian was described by the enlightened Emperor Julianus as "the Intellectual Principle," the very fount of wisdom. Her symbol was the Dove, later the symbol of the Holy Spirit.

This love and earnest respect for women was evidenced in the matriarchal Greeks. Remember their Goddesses—Palas-Athene, the Goddess of Wisdom who sprang fully armed out of the forehead of

Jove. That is to say, like all bright women with our sixth sense, intuition, which is the highest intelligence on earth, she did not need a lifetime of boring, ponderous academic analyses to know immediately what is the True, the Good and the Beautiful. The Goddess Diana the Huntress was equally athletic. The Nine Muses were female. In other words the Greeks knew that great poetry, music, history, drama sprang from the wisdom and golden imagination of women.

There were not startling physical differences between men and women then. The statue of the Winged Victory of Samothrace had not knock-knees, poor musculature nor enormous exaggerated breasts. There is a beautiful statue of Orestes and Electra who were brother and sister, their arms over each other's shoulders. They are the same height, built identically alike with the same limber prowess and athletic beauty.

The same is true of Egyptian sculpture. The Pharaohs and their queens are almost exactly alike. Even their breasts are about the same. Secondary sex characteristics that we now consider masculine and feminine came about through centuries of artificial selection due to masculine domination. This is wrong and very sad.

Many matriarchal societies have existed in which there was the opposite, female domination over men, though masculine historians have suppressed this and cannot bear to think it. Nevertheless, they existed and still do in some places. In Ancient Egypt, Diodorus Siculus tells us the women ruled their husbands. There is no ambiguity about it; the wives were absolutely supreme. Herodotus said: "With them the women discharged all kinds of public affairs. The men dealt with domestic affairs. Men were not allowed to undertake service or any of the functions of government. Nor were they allowed to fill any public office, which might have given them more spirit to set themselves against women. The children were handed over immediately after birth to the men, who reared them on milk." In Sparta women were the dominant sex. They alone could own property. This was the case among the Iroquois, the Kamchadales in Siberia, and countless others. "When women ruled in Kamchatka, the men not only did the cooking but all the housework, docilely doing everything assigned to them," according to the historian C. Meiners. "Men are so domesticated that they greatly dislike being away from home for more than one day. Should a longer absence than this become necessary, they try to persuade their wives to accompany them, for they cannot get on without the women folk.

"There was only one way in which members of the exploring party in Kamchatka could bribe the Kamchatkan women to undertake tasks regarded by them with contempt (men's work). This was by gratification of their sexual appetite. The point is worth noting because it is so characteristic of mono-sexual domination to find the dominating sex repaying the subordinate sex for sexual services. When men rule, it is the way of men to reward women for their caresses, and the practice, of course, tends to degenerate into prostitution. Where women rule we find the reverse of this tendency: women reward men for the gifts of love."

This is why in a Men's State like ours, men despise feminine tasks. Note that with us, women are proud when they can do men's work. No woman would be offended to be a Justice of the Supreme Court, just as an Ancient Egyptian would be proud of himself if he—even little he— could do a woman's work, that is, be a tall, swashbuckling soldier.

In Abyssinia, in Lapland, men did what seems to us women's work. Tacitus, describing the early Teutons, tells how women did all the work, the hunting, tilling the soil, while men idled and looked after the house, equivalent now to playing bridge and taking naps. The heirlooms in the family, a harnessed horse, a strong spear, a sword and shield, passed on to the women. They were the fighters.

And so they were in Libya, in the Congo. In India under the Queens of Nepal only women soldiers were known. In Dahomey, (now Benin), the king had a bodyguard of warrior women and these were braver than any of his men warriors and would reproach each other for cowardice or weakness with such phrases as, "You are a woman!" And physiologically, things were reversed: the women, more active and strenuous, became taller, stronger, tougher than the sedentary homebody men. Now I do not approve of this. I consider it as unhealthy, as disgusting as our own state of affairs, our exaggerated inequality.

Robert Graves says the greatest civilizations were matriarchal. But the ancient Hebrew were patriarchal, very anti-woman, with their stern, tetchy, male God, Jehovah. And so were the Romans for the most part, expressing their dominant masculinity in Law and War. But the Mycenaean Greeks and the Etruscans were matriarchal; far better civilizations, more graceful, gifted, and kind.

The Semitic race, Hebrews, Islam, all degraded women. They were obsessed with the idea of an all-male God and the superiority of the male sex. Moses and Abraham—in fact there is a persistent ungentlemanliness, a lack of feeling of justice and kindliness toward women, in the Old Testament. They were so terribly concerned with breeding, concubines and herds. Instead of kind, mighty and beautiful Goddesses, they had one harsh, punishing He-man God. I have a friend who says: "if only the Lord's Prayer had been, 'Our Mother who are in Heaven…' all would have been different."

The obsession infiltrated into Christianity through Paul. And note how the three great monotheisms, Judaism, Mohammedanism, and Christianity have produced power-loving, aggressive people, revering masculine qualities with their constant wars, the subjugation of women (women, remember, were unfairly handicapped in this contest by having a child a year). They have tragically lacked the moral attributes of the Wisdom Goddess, love, mercy, purity, wisdom, and compassion. They have, in fact, been worshipping a semi-Deity, half a God. And so the world has arrived at its present state. We cannot deny that it is the worst half.

The divinely balanced nature, man *and* woman, together and equal, was manifested in Jesus. He was on our side. His power was restricted to ideas of compassion, healing and mercy and never applied to coercion and punishment.

Now women emerged somewhat in the Renaissance with the rediscovery of Greek culture. It flowered with excitement—a passion for learning and the nations of the great pagans. It became fashionable for kings and nobility to give their children, BOTH girls and boys, into the care of the greatest men of the day, like Erasmus. Vittorino da Feltre,

149

teaching the children of the Dukes of Urbino, created three generations of wonderful men and women. You see the GIRLS were included. And great women to appear, Vittoria da Colonna whom Michelangelo loved, Caterina Sforza the soldier, St. Catherine of Sienna, the great teacher and stateswoman. I am sure that Joan of Arc was a Renaissance manifestation. Shakespeare's women show this—wonderful women "learned, kind and fair" as he said of Sylvia. There was Portia, Beatrice, Cordelia, even Lady Macbeth had a little ability and courage—bright stars appearing suddenly out of fourteen dark centuries when women were sub-nobodies. Indeed, as they are now.

Then came the Reformation and Martin Luther—closed down the magnificent ideas of antiquity and kicked women back into the kitchen. And there we have stayed since the days of Susan B. Anthony.

Now about our physical inferiority. We have seen how the dominating sex gets bigger and stronger, but this is very dysgenic, the opposite of eugenic, and very hard on us all, the whole race. To feel superior, men chose wives with low-grade physical prowess, unable to walk or run decently, with feeble feet, ruined knees, and, as at present, enormously exaggerated breasts (a masculine predilection promoted now by that absurd monster, Hugh Hefner). Their offspring, of course, dwindle and become inferior. "A little woman as high as my heart," was the tender phrase. And men chose such women, as Bertrand Russell said, "because it makes them feel so big and strong without incurring any real danger."

Fear of bugs and thunder was adorable and it is still considered so, when it should arouse in men fierce scorn. Courage is the greatest virtue, because unless you have it, you cannot practice any of the other virtues. The fraidy-cat mother inflicts a terrible psychic handicap on her sons. Among wild animals the newly born offspring has no fear at all until he sees it in his mother. Men with instinctive fears because of cowardly mothers have to hide it all their lives, a cause of terrible mental suffering and breakdown.

Now why do women not yet amount to much? Hardly a hundred years ago, what was our lot? A child a year. (Incidentally, not much time to write Shakespeare's plays, to compose symphonies.) No education. (When the University of Wisconsin allowed girls to recite in class with boys, there was a terrible uproar.) Not allowed to vote. To own property. To own our own children. Why didn't we keep away from marriage then? Because there was only one alternative—prostitution. In the Civil War they needed women as schoolteachers, so they gave the girls a little education. Fifty years later, they needed typists and girls who could work in offices.

We had very poor health. Heavily corseted. Skirts fourteen feet around the bottom and dragging in the mud. No exercise at all, not allowed to "romp," as the saying was. This induced chronic ailing, headaches, the vapors, ten days a month of acute menstrual sickness. (This was one of the big arguments against woman suffrage.)

Sargent at Harvard wondered why girls were such poor stuff athletically. Girls and boys under 13 were structurally identical, agile and lively. But after that girls were clapped in iron corsets and lost three inches in length of their thighs. No circulation. Thereafter they were weak and clumsy.

Considering these things we have not done so badly.

Now I come to a generalization. We, the women, do not have to worry about being kind. Our maternal physiology accounts for this. We are kind already and cannot help it. It is men who must worry about that. They must worry about their hardness, their dry know-it-allism, their destructiveness. (If any men in the audience have been lucky enough to inherit equally from their mothers, I do not mean you.) That is why I want an honorable equality.

For millennia, mothers have pampered their male children with the result that husbands are dreadfully aggrieved if they have not wives solely focused on their small achievements. Note that women admire men for their first-rate equalities. Men admire women *not* for their bravery, their intelligence, their contributions to society, but for their splendid courage in baking cookies for themselves.

Do not think our liberation has arrived. Just consider our unimportance. Being women, we abhor war—babies of 18 and 19 killed by the tens of thousands, for no reason at all. And we abhor just as much the killing by hundreds of thousands of slim little Asian boys and girls, living on a little rice, who heroically hurl themselves into death because they want their own country (Vietnam). (Note that, this aspect of the wars seems not to bother men too much.) Half of this country is women. The war goes right on. What women think is as powerless as a sigh, a breath, a vapor. Look at TV. Only men: soldiers, politicians, commentators...football players, coaches. No women. Oh yes, now and then one of those singers moaning about love. Or some narcissistic idiot applying hair spray. If women were equal, half the postmen, policemen, truck drivers, welders, air pilots, doctors, lawyers would be women, half of Congress, the judges and so on. Why not? I think half the soldiers should be women. This will be good because women are less docile than men and will tear up their draft cards in a fury; and probably go to the front and beat the tar out of all the soldiers of *both* armies: "Get out of here! Quit it! Go home, where you belong!"

Smedley Butler, a fierce cussing Major General of the US Marines in World War II, was a Quaker and a pacifist. After the war he went all over making speeches. "What the hell is the matter with you, you blank-blank women, that you allow it...letting these babies of 18 and 19 go to war!" I feel that way all the time. I wonder about it.

That is why we must have equal power in our society. We want to foster life, not coerce and destroy it. Every year twenty million American men go hunting, not from necessity, not for food, indeed at great expense, but for FUN. They kill more than a billion animals weaker than themselves, helpless. Women do not. And note that what we despise most is the unchivalry of it. Hunters are so cozily safe themselves.

That is why George Bernard Shaw said that one half of every governing body in the world MUST be women. To assure this, it will be necessary at first that every man elected has a female counterpart who goes into office with him.... Indeed we have not much time left to save this unhappy planet.

Men are loosening the bonds of women a little bit but they are almost hysterical with fear lest she exceed them in capacity and

152

achievement. They must encourage her to work, but not to excel. They hold on to their superiority with all their might. They are afraid she might be portrayed as morally and spiritually superior for that might lead to the long-suppressed realization that she is really quite first rate, maybe even a higher creature. She must therefore be dragged down and exposed as a near-animal, her worth being assessed by "vital statistics," her aim to titillate and degrade men.

Rev. W. Hayes, a Unitarian minister in England writes: "Biologists tell us that woman has been the pioneer of progress from the beginning. In the upward path from the lower species, she has led the way—in the decrease of hairiness, in the upright gait, in the shape of the head and face and jaw. Woman is the civilizer. It is through woman that a sense of human nobility and possible beauty and greatness is awakened in man." And the Irish poet AE wrote: "Woman may again have her temples and mysteries and renew again her radiant life as its fountain. Who shall save us anew shall come divinely as a woman." And our good friend Robert Graves says this, and it is so remarkable that he should be able to see it: "A real woman" he says—he points out that the word "real" is the same word as "royal"—"A real woman neither despises nor worships men, but is proud not to have been born a man, knows the full extent of her powers and feels free to reject all arbitrary man-made obligations. She is her own oracle of right and wrong, firmly believing in her own five senses and the intuitive sixth."

"Since she never settles for the second best in love, what troubles her is the rareness of real men. Real women are royal women; the word once had some meaning. Democracy has no welcome for queens. To reach some understanding of real women, one must think back to the primitive age when men invariably treated women as the holier sex because they perpetuated the race. Women were the guardians of spring, fruit trees, and the sacred hearth fire. Tribal queens judged each case on merit, not by legal code, as real women do; and showed little regard for trade and mechanical invention."

Men should be happy because women will rescue us from Science, that horrible idolatry, from dry, hard analyses, the gross literalists and

153

computers of everything. From the dry horrors of technology, bombs, automobiles, mass production and from those silly literal-minded, unloving mechanical fellows, those boring engineering scientific fellows, and measurers collecting rocks on the moon.

Women have almost no friends among men—we are always loved for the wrong thing—only a few very great ones, Pythagoras, Plato, Sophocles, Shakespeare, John Stuart Mill, Ibsen, Bernard Shaw. It seems to me one of the best ways to be a great man would be to be a true friend of women. You would be in good company. How? Neither pamper nor exploit them. Love in women their greatness, which is the same as it is in men. Insist on bravery, honor, grandeur, generosity in women.

And as for men, they should be kinder. Quit their silly mass-murdering, their conceit based on nothing, and their absolutely permeating, unstanchable infantilism, feeling wronged if all women's force and strength is not devoted to themselves, usually their weaknesses, their babyism.

I say this because I think there is a state of great unhappiness between us. If we can be true equals, we will be better friends, better lovers, better wives and husbands.

❧ *Address and sermon given at the First Unitarian Society in Minneapolis on March 7, 1971, and later at the University of Minnesota, the University of Wisconsin, and Augsburg College in Minneapolis*

↵ *Beauty Will Save the World* ↳

MY FATHER CAME from Norway to Minneapolis when he was 17, dug the Washington Avenue sewer, and became a lawyer when he was 26. My mother was born in Ohio during the Civil War among Abolitionists rescuing runaway slaves. She went to high school in Minneapolis and although very poor, she had great beauty and style. After high school she taught Sixth Grade; and years later, one of her pupils told me: "I was never bright until I was in your mother's class, and I have been bright ever since."

154

My parents were political idealists, feminists, democrats. They wanted their children to be light-hearted and athletic, to live outdoors and eat oranges and apples. My mother thought the girls should not be the menials of the boys, and so the boys made their own beds and the girls were on the football team in the pasture. She thought that if mothers were what they should be, surrounding their children with every freedom and happiness and cheerful intelligence, we would have the Millennium in one generation. She taught the baby how to hold and smooth the cat. She never cautioned us. We could walk endless miles in the country, swim across the lake, ride bareback. She would have liked Blake's aphorism: "Prudence is a rich, ugly Old Maid courted by Incapacity."

Now my wonderful parents raised us in the Unitarian Church. Did Unitarianism add to our grandeur and wisdom? I think it did. We grew up more lighthearted and untrammeled than Orthodox children, overawed and inculcated with guilt (Original Sin). The hopeless naughtiness of that—always having to drag Original Sin around! I think we were just as benign and good as the others, perhaps more so—more original, easier laughter, allowed to even have a little engaging rascality.

And my parents were generous to all religions—all of us poor humans groping in the darkness toward Eternity. The only thing wrong about Orthodoxy, they thought, was the grimness, the fraidy-catism, the self-righteous conceit, always trying to discipline others.

My mother and my brother Torvald were having a little religious conversation and he said, "Is God a bird?"

This shows that there was not much religious alarm in the family. We never said our prayers and no one told us how. The neighbor children had to say at night that frightening and dismal prayer, "If I should die before I wake...." And it was only when I heard people speak of church and religion and show their distressing tinted cards of Jesus and his disciples traipsing barefoot in their nightgowns, that I became scared of graves, dead bodies, sin and Hell and other horrors, quite unnecessary.

An interesting thing is that entirely unadmonished I became religious myself, quite cheerfully and naturally so. And whenever great men and women reveal in their lives and works their souls—Tolstoy, Blake, Carlyle, Bach, Michelangelo, Mozart, St. Joan, St. Catherine of Sienna—there expands in me a kind of light and recognition. I seem to see farther into the mysterious gloom—perhaps not so gloomy after all.

My anxiety is that Unitarians will become only Science Idolaters. Perhaps God *IS* becoming a bird to them—not a nice live bird but a stuffed bird. An electric bird, a gasohol bird. In fact I like science less and less. Isn't it Intellectual Pride? Maybe it's Lucifer after all. See how they are always measuring and counting, and what's so wonderful about that? Usually it is merely utilitarian and destructive—weaponry and herbicides, shots for cancer that don't work, more computers, more concrete on meadows, faster and more terrible airplanes looking exactly those fiends that great Dante saw in his genius and appalling imagination. No. Science may be the Tree of Death. Where is the love and beauty of it?

Just the other day in that remarkable periodical that costs 25 cents a year, the *Catholic Worker*, I discovered that both Dostoevsky and the great Russian theologian Berdynev said exactly the same thing: "Beauty will save the world."

I believe it. Please remember that and make a note of it.

❧ *Excerpted from a 1981 speech to the First Unitarian Society of Minneapolis*

৩ Blessed Are the Debonair ৩

THE FRENCH SAY things so beautifully. In French a son is mon fils, my son. But a son-in-law is mon beau fils, my *handsome* son.

Another thought: The English Bible says, "Blessed are the meek." Alas, I despise meekness and cannot bear it. (I think we should all be great kings and queens – that is the vision to have about one's self.) But in the French Bible the word for meek is debonair. "Blessed are the

156

debonair." That expresses what is meant so much better. Not Meek but debonair, flexible, blithe, light-hearted, open, free. Suggestible, so that great ideas can enter you. I like that. That is the ticket.

About being kings and queens, my father translated Bjornson's poem to Ole Gabriel Ueland [Brenda's grandfather]. The last three verses are:

> *He sank beneath the standard*
> *While striving further on,*
> *Therefore by strong valkyries*
> *He was carried to their home.*
>
> *From chilly winter evening*
> *They onward grandly led him*
> *To the lighted Hall of Saga*
> *And toward the Chief's high bench.*
>
> *Then up rose many an old lord*
> *And forward stepped to greet him,*
> *And first of all King Sverre*
> *With whom he was of kin.*

I was eating in our kitchen and Inga was at the sink washing dishes. Inga is one of us, a member of the Ueland clan in Norway. She had been our cook (boss) for thirty years. I said:

"Inga, do you think it's true that we are descended from the Kings of Norway?"

She wheeled on me fiercely.

"Brenda, don't laugh! That's true! Mr. Ueland had that kingy feeling, Mrs. Taylor (my sister Anne) has that kingy feeling and," with inexpressible hauteur, "I have it!"

The truth is that everybody in the world should have the kingy feeling: pride, honor, strength, nobility. As for my sister, Anne Taylor, she once went to see my remarkable clairvoyant friend, Maybelle

Fahstrom, who could see with her "third eye" angels, archangels, your ancestors, the future, the past. Maybelle (St. Maybelle of Upton Avenue South I called her) at once "saw" that Anne had been a great duchess. "She was the Duchess of Gloucester in another incarnation but this time she's slumming in the Ueland family."

❧ *Excerpted from the* Minnesota Posten *(October 1977)*

↩ *On Writing* ↪

"He Whose Face Gives No Light Shall Never Become a Star"
—BLAKE

WHY URGE everybody to write when the world is so full of writers, and there are oceans of printed matter?

Well, all of it does not amount to very much and little is worth remembering. Every two or three years a book comes out and everyone likes it very much and praises it and says it is a true work of art. And for these books I am grateful. But there could be a great deal more living literature, that really talks to people and does not just kill time for them.

And what is a little book or two, when there is so much greatness in the world hidden all around us? These good things that appear in print seem so meager, so slight, so publisher-touted, in this country of a hundred million people. Now one or two little books—making an impression for two years, forgotten utterly in five—that is not enough, when you think what there might be, what might come out of people.

But if (as I wish) everybody writes and respects and loves writing, then we would have a nation of intelligent, eager, impassioned readers; and generous and grateful ones, not mere critical, logy, sedentary passengers, observers of writing, whose attitude is: "All right: entertain me now." Then we would all talk to each other in our writing with excitement and passionate interest, like free men and brothers, and like the people in paradise, whom Dostoevsky described

158

in a story: "not only in their songs but in all their lives they seemed to do nothing but admire each other." The result: some great, great national literature.

And this is all that I have to say.

To sum up—if you want to write:

- Know that you have talent, are original and have something   important to say.
- Know that it is good to work. Work with love and think   of liking it when you do it. It is easy and interesting. It is a privilege. There is nothing hard about it but your anxious vanity and fear of failure.
- Write freely, recklessly, in first drafts.
- Tackle anything you want to—novels, plays, anything. Only remember Blake's admonition: "Better to strangle an infant in its cradle than to nurse unacted desires."
- Don't be afraid of writing bad stories. To discover what is wrong with a story write two new ones and then go back to it.
- Don't fret or be ashamed of what you have written in the past. How I always suffered from this! How I would regurgitate out of my memory (and still do) some nauseous little lumps of things I had written! But don't do this. Go on to the next. And fight against this tendency, which is much of it due not to splendid modesty, but a lack of self-respect. We are too ready (women especially) not to stand by what we have said or done. Often it is a way of forestalling criticism, saying hurriedly: "I know it is awful!" before anyone else does. Very bad and cowardly. It is so conceited and timid to be ashamed of one's mistakes. Of *course* they are mistakes. Go on to the next.
- Try to discover your true, honest, untheoretical self.
- Don't think of yourself as an intestinal tract and tangle of nerves in the skull that will not work unless you drink coffee. Think of yourself as incandescent power, illuminated perhaps and forever talked to by God and his messengers. Remember

159

how wonderful you are, what a miracle! Think if Tiffany's made a mosquito, how wonderful we would think it was!

- If you are never satisfied with what you write, that is a good sign. It means your vision can see so far that it is hard to come to it. Again I say, the only unfortunate people are the glib ones, immediately satisfied with their work. To them the ocean is only knee-deep.

- When discouraged, remember what Van Gogh said: "If you hear a voice within you saying: You are no painter, then paint by all means, lad, and that voice will be silenced, but only by working."

- Don't be afraid of yourself when you write. Don't check-rein yourself. If you are afraid of being sentimental, say, for heaven's sake be as sentimental as you can or feel like being! Then you will probably pass through to the other side and slough off sentimentality because you understand it at last and really don't care about it.

- Don't always be appraising yourself, wondering if you are better or worse than other writers. "I will not Reason & Compare," said Blake; "my business is to Create." Besides, since you are like no other being ever created since the beginning of Time, you are incomparable.

And why should you do all these things? Why should we all use our creative power and write or paint or play music, or whatever it tells us to do?

Because there is nothing that makes people so generous, joyful, lively, bold, and compassionate, so indifferent to fighting and accumulation of objects and money. Because the best way to know the Truth or Beauty is to try to express it. And what is the purpose of existence Here or Yonder but to discover truth and beauty and to express it, i.e., share it with others?

And so I really believe this book will hasten the Millennium by two or three hundred years. And if it has given you the impulse to

160

write one small story, then I am pleased.

❧ Excerpted from the book If You Want to Write, courtesy the Schubert Club, first published in 1938 by G.P. Putnam's Sons

✍ Our Primeval Motion ✍
A Little Philosophy About Running

MORE AND MORE people do it. It is an addiction. They cannot stop it and do not want to. The ability to run a Marathon seems to be built in. It is slowly acquired after days and months of trotting and jogging around. If you keep running, there you are—able to go 26 miles. A scholarly friend (young middle-age) now finds herself running six miles a day in one hour. And the queerest thing of all is her sorrow, indignation, when it is 20 below zero and there is a blizzard and she cannot do it. She misses it grievously. It has become a pleasure, a delight, an absolute necessity.

And here is the most mysterious, the most paradoxical thing of all: Instead of subtracting, or taking away from the sum of one's energy, it seems to double it, to quadruple it.

Why does it become such an addiction, and why cannot people stop running? I think it is perhaps our original, primeval way of motion, that it is really natural, right for us to gently run. We are then like happy deer, antelopes, wolves, wild horses. Running is the way we *should* move. And for miles.

And please remember the awful experience Americans have been through for two generations: riding in cars. From here to New York and from here to the drugstore. You make a rather inadequate parking effort with your car and you say apologetically to your passenger: "Never mind. We can walk to the curb."

I often think of man's history on earth as the round dial of a clock and say that twelve o'clock is the Year one Anno Domini, the birth of Christ. Now man has existed on earth millions of years.

The hand of the clock indicating our year, 2,000 years, would be about a hundredth of a hair beyond twelve o'clock. It is really just an Eyewink of time, an Augenblick. And this Eyewink, our even briefer period, is the Age of Gasoline. It is our Spree on Gasoline. World Wars, Hiroshimas, airplanes, bombers, neutron bombs, H-bombs, Millions dead, billions frightened and wretched. Just think! Maybe in another Eyewink gasoline will be exhausted. All gone!

I know that when that time comes, I myself, the blue birds, the cardinals, the wild animals, the frogs, the cowslips, the naturalists, the poets, the prophets, the peacemakers will be delighted! A few darling weeds will begin to push through the ugly, sterile concrete. No more gasoline! Thank God! Hurrah, hurrah!

❀ Excerpted from the Minnesota Posten (December 1977)

✒ Like Lord Byron ❧

SOMETIMES PEOPLE complain—my children and others—that I dress so unstylishly, so eccentrically, indeed so badly. I say this: "If I did not wear torn pants, orthopedic shoes, frantic disheveled hair, that is to say, if I did not tone down my beauty, people would go mad. Married men would run amuck."

And sometimes I say this: "As a matter of fact I am so original, so inventive that I dress about 25 years ahead of the fashion. I can prove it. I was the first woman in the Western World to have my hair cut off. I went to Henri in Greenwich Village, the French barber at the Hotel Breevoort in New York, and I told him to cut my hair all off. He was frightened, appalled. To cut off that nice, very black, ladylike hair, with a pug! I described to him what I wanted. "I want it to be like Lord Byron's—as if a high wind were blowing from the rear."

He did so. It was splendid. Wherever I went seas of white faces turned to gaze. That is just what I liked.

❀ Excerpted from the Minnesota Posten (August 12, 1979)

✑ Inspiration ✑

I LEARNED... that inspiration does not come like a bolt, nor is it kinetic, energetic striving, but it comes into us slowly and quietly and all the time, though we must regularly and every day give it a little chance to start following, prime it with a little solitude and idleness. I learned that you should feel when writing, not like Lord Byron on a mountain top, but like a child stringing beads in kindergarten—happy, absorbed and quietly putting one bead on after another.

❧ *Excerpted from the book* If You Want to Write, *courtesy the Schubert Club, first published in 1938 by G.P. Putnam's Sons*

✑ Bright Shoots of Everlastingness ✑

I HAVE A THEORY that music lifts the spirit from the ground to a little freedom. It is as though you float a little above yourself, and dust falls away, and what we are meant to be is there. *Jakob Böhme* said that Eternity is that flash of time when we are what we love. And music does that—"The bright shoots of everlastingness."

❧ *Excerpted from* Mitropoulos and the North High Band, *1983, courtesy the Schubert Club, St. Paul*

✑ Pulled Two Ways at Once ✑

ALL MY LIFE I seem to have had two forces working in me—pushing me, making me search, search and never rest. They give me an energy that sets my mind wrangling and struggling and arguing and discussing things, whenever I am alone. One energy seems to be the wish to be important and admired. The other energy is that I want to *be* what is admirable inside, whether anyone admires me or not. And this passion grows as the other one wanes.

They have a kind of rhythm. I sometimes describe it by saying that for two weeks I seem to be my father and for two weeks my mother. That is, for two weeks I want to be bold and remarkable, and this fills me with energy for a while. But then suddenly, almost in a few minutes, I will think: "Oh no, to be good, unselfish is the thing. How obnoxious, how meaty, empty and egotistical, all that masculine striving!" And I want to be graceful and tender—even to have ringlets and wear lace blouses—to be a listener, and a fosterer of others and all life.

❦ *Excerpted from* Me, *courtesy the Schubert Club, first published in 1939 by G.P. Putnam's Sons*

✍ *Beauty and Bravery* ✎

HEALTH IS NOT A HUMDRUM, inconsequential thing that means you are able to get to the office and stay out of the hospital. The word "health" means also "whole" and "holy." And you cannot have beauty and bravery and grandeur and exuberance, generosity and joviality and a kind of affectionate fearlessness unless you have health. Nor indeed can you be really sane.

Now the queer thing is that you can have it if you want it, although you must know how, and that is what I am going to tell you. But remember this: Health, like Freedom, must be won every day. You have to exert yourself in a lively and dauntless way throughout your whole life in order to get it.

A great deal is known about it. Doctors know less about it than almost anyone and what I say is going to throw them and thousands of people in a rage. Great people from Hippocrates and Plato to Michelangelo and Tolstoy, Gandhi, George Bernard Shaw, Swedenborg, knew what health was and how to achieve it, although so far none of them has discovered how to stay alive on this earth forever...

Now the interesting thing is this: While doctors disagree about why we are sick in so many hundreds of various ways, these great wise

164

ones whom I have just mentioned, who knew so much about health, all agree about the causes of it and virtually recommend the same thing if you want to achieve it...

I had the most remarkable and wonderful mother. When she married my father she was very slender, albeit beautiful and intelligent. Somebody predicted that she would not live two years, she seemed so finely spun and delicate. But she lived and had eight children. I never heard her utter a cross or irritated or unkind word and, without obvious, nervous strenuosity, she accomplished wonders, among other things woman suffrage for the State of Minnesota and the United States, one of their most eminent leaders. She worked serenely sixteen hours a day, finding time to take long solitary walks and to read to her children in relays, Shakespeare to the older ones and Dickens and Sir Walter Scott to the younger.

She had ideas about health. Nobody else seemed to give it a thought in those times. Girls and women were tightly corseted. They were not allowed "to romp." They dragged heavy skirts fourteen feet around the bottom in the mud, wore layers of starched underwear and thick black stockings.

We had a large white house on Lake Calhoun in Minneapolis and four green and wooded acres. My mother had the absurd and unheard of notion that sunlight and air were good for us. She put me in the sun as a baby, so browned that Mr. Emmanuel Cohen called me "The Eskimo." I remember my pretty little brother Rolf, four years old, walking under the elm trees and in the checkered sunlight, naked like Cupid, with golden ringlets. We swam in the lake, across the lake and back, like dolphins. We went barefoot in order to have plump and perfect feet like quattrocento angels...

Fridtjof Nansen had grave misgivings about "urbanization." This was happening even in Norway. When I saw him in 1929 he spoke of it sadly. There had always been the sturdy, independent and fearless farmer-people of Norway, each one a kind of bold, truth-telling democratic king on his own rocky little farm, with his plow, his few cows and goats going up to the high mountain pastures in summer, his boat going out on the glassy fjord or to the wild sea to fish. These healthy fresh-faced people were being drawn, charmed into the cities by regular wages, and heated offices. He was afraid they would not only lose their proud separateness and sturdiness but their great health, their tirelessness at work, their splendid physiques with broad shoulders, wide chests and straight long legs.

Of course this has happened all over the world. In England, the stature of Scottish laborers who went into English factories dropped five inches in a generation. We know the story of the swollen cities in the United States, the starving family farms.

When Nansen was honored at St. Andrews University in Edinburgh the title of his Rectorial Address to the Scotch students was "Adventure."

"You will find your Adventure," he said, "for life itself is an adventure. Everyone should try to hit upon his own trail. Do not lose your opportunities, and do not allow yourself to be carried away by the superficial rush and scramble which is modern life.

"The first thing is to find yourself, and for that you need solitude and contemplation, at least sometimes. I tell you deliverance will not come from the rushing, noisy centers of civilization. It will come from the lonely places. The great reformers in history have come from the wilderness.

"My friend, Knud Rasmussen, the Danish explorer, told me a remarkable story about a medicine man and conjurer of the primitive Eskimo of the Barren Grounds of Northern Canada. This simple savage who had hardly ever seen a white man, said to his friend and colleague, Rasmussen: 'The true wisdom is found far from men, out in the great solitude, and can only be obtained through suffering. Privation and suffering are the only road to wisdom, and they alone can open a man's mind for that which is hidden to others.'

"He went on to describe how, in order to become a sage, a man had to fast fourteen days in an unheated snow-hut at the coldest time

166

Brenda, flanked by her sisters Elsa (left) and Anne (right), ca. 1893.

Brenda in the backyard of her Stamford, Connecticut home, circa 1928.

The Ueland family and friends, circa 1896. Brenda is
in the middle, holding the pony's bridle.

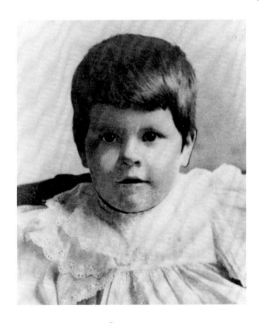

Brenda's dark hair
and eyes inspired her
childhood nickname,
"The Eskimo."

Brenda, on the shore of Lake Calhoun, Minneapolis circa 1935 advised
everyone to "walk well and grandly, with grace... the point is not to live
long... we live forever anyway. The point is while you are alive be alive."

XII

Brenda's friend the author and fashion illustrator Grace Hart,
a.k.a. Tomola, on the roof of her Park Avenue penthouse

Brenda and Gaby, circa 1926.

Brenda with her third husband,
the Norwegian American artist
Sverre Hanssen, circa 1960.

Brenda circa 1930.   Brenda circa 1940.

"I am so original, so inventive that I dress about 25 years ahead of the fashion... I was the first woman in the Western World to have my hair cut off. I went to Henri in Greenich Village... and told him to cut my hair off. He was frightened, apalled... 'I want it to be like Lord Byron's — as if a high wind were blowing from the rear.' It was splendid. Wherever I went seas of white faces turned to gaze. That is just what I liked."

XIV

Brenda in Greenwich Village, 1929.

Brenda circa 1938

Brenda circa 1945

Brenda Ueland at 90, in 1981. "Death's a joke", she said.
I can hardly wait— all those nice souls over yonder."

XVI

in the middle of winter. Then comes another medicine man with a drink of hot water and a little raw meat. And after that the man has to go on fasting as long as he possibly can. He should never finish his struggle for wisdom."

But most people, Nansen said, "are satisfied too soon and that is the reason why there is so little wisdom in the world..." And so few, so few great men and women! Leaders! We absolutely must have them!

He said that it is doubtful if there is any superiority in so-called "civilized man." "Go back 6000 years and the ancient Egyptians accomplished miracles with their simple implements and their great intelligence. How can we feel ourselves superior to them?

"If we go still further back – some twelve or fifteen thousand years – we find Cro-Magnon people. With magnificent stature, taller than we are, perhaps six feet three inches in height, and what skulls! Look at the beautiful high arch from the forehead to the base of the skull! A cranium with one-sixth more brain than that of a modern European...

"Oh no, my friends. The rising trend of evolution stopped thousands of years ago, owing to the condition of modern social life, especially in its urbanization, which makes the inferior elements of mankind so prolific. The human race is certainly changing, but it is no use galloping if you are going in the wrong direction."

He thought that a fundamental evil in urbanization is that there is never again any true solitude, no prolonged loneliness. In that loneliness there lies illumination and vision and bright strength and courage. And as he found it skiing in the wildest mountains of Norway, here again I bring forward my earnest argument: that at least you can walk, and walk alone for miles and miles and day after day.

This in our day is the only absolute guarantee of thought, of your own thought, not the thoughts of others, or the scattered, nervous, multitudinous thoughts of books, newspapers, professors, parents, ministers and politicians...

Another interesting and gallant Norwegian, an athlete and hero, was Colonel Ole Reistad. When the German Grand Fleet steamed up the Oslofjord that black April night, he was the Commander of 14 airplanes so antique that he called them "a flying museum." German Messerschmitts cluttered the whole sky. The Flying Museum did its tiny best, retreating northward towards Narvik. Then Ole Reistad crossed Siberia and came to America. Norwegian boys joined him there, some coming in rowboats across the North Sea. He trained the Royal Norwegian Air Force in Canada. We know its achievements with the R.A.F.

In Norway he as a pre-eminent athlete, the winner of the Egeberg Trophy. Three times during the war he came to Minneapolis and here are some notes about him that I wrote then:

November 1943. He has recently been made a Colonel although he said, "No. I am a Major. Norway is where they fight. No one must go back to Norway with more titles than he had before."

When he arrived at the Minneapolis airport he was bare-headed. He loves the sun. He has a blazing sunburn and his yellow hair and eyebrows are as bright as gilt. I cannot keep him indoors: When reporters and others come to interview him he makes them sit outdoors with him on the western lawn. The rest of us feel a little uneasy when we are not warm and stuffy in the house but he seems to feel comfortable only out under the sky.

When it was time to take him downtown for his speech on the radio, there he was on the lawn running figure-eights in tennis shoes and shorts. Earlier in the morning when I came down to breakfast Selma was looking uneasily out the dining-room windows at Lake Calhoun, grey and wolfish with the north wind. "He went swimming!"...

...In 1944 I asked him about his family. His wife was in Norway, quietly starving under the Nazis and risking her life in the Underground. He showed me her picture with smiling eagerness – a short nose, yellow hair, a wide-stretched smile. "She is very saucy," he said admiringly. He had two boys aged ten and twelve.

"What will they be when they grow up?"

"Farmers of course," he said. "Every other generation must return and become farmers again. Farmers do the hardest work. They become straightforward, independent. That is their greatness. If people are more than one generation in cities, in offices – lawyers, businessmen, professors – courage goes. They become nervous, indirect crafty. This is not good...."

⸙ Excerpted from Brenda Ueland's unpublished book, *Beauty and Bravery*:

᠂᠊ᢌ *On Making Choices* ᢀᢌ

THE CHOICES turn up every few minutes, every hour. "To be or not to be?" To choose bravery or flight? To choose your natural carefree, rollicking self, to choose your cautious, pussyfooting self?

This making of choices I have mulled over all my life. My thought is that if your choices are lofty, noble, daring, perhaps even dangerous, the line of your life will go along a higher level than, say, if your choices are lazier, more self-indulgent, cozy and imitative. Your choices determine whether your life will go along at a distinguished noble level or a lower level—duller, more namby-pamby. Or the level may be very low indeed—in the mud. Or it may be an opportunistic, crass, vulgar level.

We must try to make wonderful choices. Now this is not easy. For one reason, we don't know who we are. As Boethius, the philosopher and Christian martyr of the 5th Century, said to his torturers: "You have forgotten who you are."

I feel that I am about seventeen people. How to single out one's True Self? I seem to be sometimes my mother, sometimes my father, sometimes a whiner, a great queen, or a slob, a mother, a simpering lady or an old rip, a minister, a lion, a weasel. I have this concept: We are like onions, in layers. Many people live from the outer layer of the onion. They live in what other people think is the thing to do. They are merely imitative or conventional. Their Conscience is that still small voice that tells them someone is looking.

169

But we must try to find our True Conscience, our True Self, the very Center, for this is the only first-rate choice-making center. Here lies all originality, talent, honor, truthfulness, courage and cheerfulness. Here only lies the ability to choose the good and the grand, the true and the beautiful.

But how to find your Center? It is very hard in our cacophonous times; fractured with yelling activity, feeding, drinking, galloping, of frantic uncertainties that lead to psychiatry and booze. But you must try to find it. It is the old stuff—Know Thyself. But it takes solitude and there is none. I knew a remarkable woman who had a famous boys' school and she made them, every so often, watch the sheep alone and all night. A good idea. Gandhi's rule, like that of all the saints, was to be silent for twenty-four hours one day a week—not to utter one word. Then one was bound to look inward and the Center begins to appear. To find it you must ask yourself all the time: "What do I love? Why am I irascible? Why am I so afraid of old age and death? How odd, for both seem to be very common. Maybe I should not be afraid of them."

Now when you find this Center, or as you approach it, it is much easier to make choices. But here I must say that Unitarians may drive me out of the fold for heresy. I am a Unitarian but I am not a Humanist at all but a fantastical mystic. I must tell you that, with Plato, I think the purpose of life on earth is, "the tendance of the soul," that is to say, we are in school. And like Plato, I believe in the Doctrine of Reminiscence or Reincarnation, and that in this life we are supposed to learn something, to advance, to become better. As in Ibsen's mystical drama, *Peer Gynt*, I think our soul, or Solveig, is waiting for us at the end of life and hopes that we have passed with a good mark and have learned something through striving, mistakes, suffering and the like.

And therefore I believe that our choices should not be practical and pragmatic, founded on business achievements in the world, or success, or public acclaim, but we should try to make choices in the direction of nobility and bravery, if possible.

Now some of us do not want to be noble. Fine. If your True Self says, "Don't be noble," don't be. But if it says, "Be noble," and you want to be that that, you will go insane or have a nervous breakdown if you don't make those choices. Now since our Conscience is a tiny compass inside us, our duty is to keep this little compass as sensitive and imaginative as possible, clear and alive, to keep it as nervously steady as possible.

How to do that? Two generations ago solitude was a normal part of every life. Now it hardly exists. There is not even the solitude of walking, of going from here to here on our legs.

Some people try to live up to a Conscience higher than their own, say that of Jesus or Calvin. A terrible mistake and it accounts for the persecutions and cruelties of Christianity, and the suffering of endless generations of children. For one thing, it can't be done. Because the Conscience of many people tells them to be quite ordinary, eating, drinking, fighting and having a good time, but their artificially assumed Conscience won't allow it and it makes them not only dreadful and cruel, but idiotic.

Now in making choices, never be grim. Think of life as a river, a smooth-following, golden Heraclitean river. Know that you will make dreadful mistakes with almost every choice. Hurrah! Congratulate yourself for daring, honorable, ridiculous mistakes. Children are so terribly afraid their parents will prevent them from making their most important mistakes.

There are tests to submit your choices to. Tolstoy said that a great man is one who has the highest Life Conception of his time. Well, I say to myself: "What is *my* Highest Life Conception?" I make myself define it, describe it. Or I say to myself, "In this trying situation, what would God do?" Hamlet should have asked himself that. The answer would have come immediately. "Don't kill Claudius. Or your mother. Be kinder to Ophelia. Don't fake madness. Intelligently plan the overthrow of Claudius and establish a good administration."

The original great test for choices was the Ten Commandments. Still very good. Although some of us think that we have transcended some of them, like this one, "Honor thy father and mother." Well this is an anachronism. You can be wonderfully good to them but you cannot honor them if they are not honorable. My friend, Ammon Hennacy, a Catholic and a religious anarchist who breaks the law in every war and goes to jail, said to the shocked policeman who arrested him: "An anarchist is a person who is too good to need a policeman."

Jesus's two commandments, "Love thy God with all thy heart and mind, and thy neighbor as thyself," are helpful. Although a young philosopher said that to do unto others as you would be done by "would be rather catastrophic in a society of masochists." George Bernard Shaw had an even better commandment, as an advance on that of Moses and Jesus. It is: "Is this that I enjoy doing for twenty minutes hurting any man or creature in the world?"

I have my own two commandments to propose to the world and curiously enough they are not stressed in the Bible; they are not even included in the Seven Deadly Sins. They are: No Cruelty. And no Lying.

That would take care of everything—ignorance-inducing newspapers, advertising, war, stealing, murder, vivisection, adultery. For example, the true viciousness of adultery is not the romantic love —there is no objection to Tristan and Isolde—but the cruelty and the lying, for lying is so bad for the liar and it is such an injustice and cruelty to the person lied to.

And if my two commandments prevailed there would emerge a world without psychiatrists, salesmen and nervous breakdowns.

Another important test for choices in ethics and morals is aesthetic. Beauty is the Lord. Cowardice is ugly and plug-ugly. So is tyranny and exploitation, the stronger bludgeoning the weaker. So is lying ugly. Chekhov said that lying is dirty and that it is even worse to lie in fiction than in conversation. Snobbishness is so disgustingly unlovely, such an indication of pin-headedness. Caterwauling and self-pity—such a revolting sight for human eyes!

If protesting against censorship nobody points out that works of sexual freedom are often so extraordinarily ugly. And ugliness is an infection, a pestilential thing. It invades people; just as Beauty heals and lightens them. It depresses them, lowers them, muddies them, changes them for the worse. Ugliness is Devil Worship. This should be a test for modern art and music. Much of it should be prohibited.

My final admonition in making choices is: Study especially what you *think* is your goodness. Is it self-sacrifice? Being meek, long-suffering? Watch it. It may be cowardice. And the meek do so much harm. A docile, put-upon wife ruins the nature and soul of her husband. Better to knock him out with a lead pipe. There would be no tyranny if nobody would put up with it. Or do you consider your greatest virtue a piercing critical sense? Watch it. It may be self-praise, or an inability to love, or a pervading hate. Are you doing work that is profitable but ugly and shoddy and a deceiving of the public; and do you explain it by saying "One has to live." Ask yourself: "But do you?"

And never rest in any rule. No stereotypes are allowed. There is no resting place down here. George Herbert in a poem tells how at Man's birth God gave him Beauty, Courage and so on, and at the bottom of the cup was Rest. God started to give him that but put it back. "No, he can never have rest. Eternal restlessness will at last throw him to my Breast."

My conclusion is then: Avoid in your choices all cruelty and lying. After that, I say to my children, "Be Bad or Good, whichever is best for you."

And here endeth the First Lesson.

* *From Brenda Ueland's papers, the Minnesota Historical Society, courtesy the Schubert Club*

৩ Tell Me More: On the Fine Art of Listening ৬

I WANT TO WRITE about the great and powerful thing that listening is. And how we forget it. And how we don't listen to our children, or those we love. And least of all—which is so important too—to those we do not love. But we should. Because listening is a magnetic and strange thing, a creative force. Think how the friends that really listen to us are the ones we move toward, and we want to sit in their radius as though it did us good, like ultraviolet rays.

This is the reason: When we are listened to, it creates us, makes us unfold and expand. Ideas actually begin to grow within us and come to life. You know how if a person laughs at your jokes you become funnier and funnier, and if he does not, every tiny little joke in you weazens up and dies. Well, that is the principle of it. It makes people happy and free when they are listened to. And if you are a listener, it is the secret of having a good time in society (because everybody around you becomes lively and interesting), of comforting people, of doing them good.

Who are the people, for example, to whom you go for advice? Not to the hard, practical ones who can tell you exactly what to do, but to the listeners; that is, the kindest, least censorious, least bossy people that you know. It is because by pouring out your problem to them, you then know what to do about it yourself.

When we listen to people there is an alternating current, and this recharges us so that we never get tired of each other. We are constantly being re-created. Now there are brilliant people who cannot listen much. They have no ingoing wires on their apparatus. They are entertaining, but exhausting, too. I think it is because these lecturers, these brilliant performers, by not giving us a chance to talk, do not let us express our thoughts and expand; and it is this little creative foundation inside us that begins to spring up and cast up new thoughts and unexpected laughter and wisdom. That is why, when someone has listened to you, you go home rested and lighthearted.

Now this little creative fountain is in us all. It is the spirit, or the intelligence, or the imagination—whatever you want to call it. If you are very tired, strained, have no solitude, run too many errands, talk to too many people, drink too many cocktails, this little fountain is muddied over and covered with a lot of debris. The result is you stop living from the center, the creative fountain, and you live from the periphery, from externals. That is, you go along on mere will power without imagination.

174

It is when people really listen to us, with quiet fascinated attention, that the little fountain begins to work again, to accelerate in the most surprising way.

I discovered all this about three years ago, and truly it made a revolutionary change in my life. Before that, when I went to a party I would think anxiously: "Now try hard. Be lively. Say bright things. Talk. Don't let down." And when tired, I would have to drink a lot of coffee to keep this up.

Now before going to a party, I just tell myself to listen with affection to anyone who talks to me, *to be in their shoes when they talk*; to try to know them without my mind pressing against theirs, or arguing or changing the subject. No. My attitude is: "Tell me more. This person is showing me his soul. It is a little dry and meager and full of grinding talk just now, but presently he will begin to think, not just automatically to talk. He will show his true self. Then he will be wonderfully alive."

Sometimes, of course, I cannot listen as well as others. But when I have this listening power, people crowd around and their heads keep turning to me as though irresistibly pulled. It is not because people are conceited and want to show off that they are drawn to me, the listener. It is because by listening I have started up their creative fountain. I do them good.

Now why does it do them good? I have a kind of mystical notion about this. I think it is only by expressing all that is inside that purer and purer streams come. It is so in writing. You are taught in school to put down on paper only the bright things. Wrong. Pour out the dull things on paper too—you can tear them up afterward—for only then do the bright ones come. If you hold back the dull things, you are certain to hold back what is clear and beautiful and true and lively. So it is with people who have not been listened to in the right way— with affection and a kind of jolly excitement. Their creative fountain has been blocked. Only superficial talk comes out—what is prissy or gushing or merely nervous. No one has called out of them, by wonderful listening, what is true and alive.

I think women have this listening faculty more than men. It is not the fault of men. They lose it because of their long habit of striving in business, of self-assertion. And the more forceful men are, the less they can listen as they grow older. And that is why women in general are more fun than men, more restful and inspiring.

Now this non-listening of able men is the cause of one of the saddest things in the world—the loneliness of fathers, of those quietly sad men who move among their grown children like remote ghosts. When my father was over 70, he was a fiery, humorous, admirable man, a scholar, a man of great force. But he was deep in the loneliness of old age and another generation. He was so fond of me. But he could not hear me—not one word I said, really. I was just his audience. I would walk around the lake with him on a beautiful afternoon and he would talk to me about Darwin and Huxley and Higher Criticism of the Bible.

"Yes, I see, I see," I kept saying and tried to keep my mind pinned to it, but I was restive and bored. There was a feeling of helplessness because he could not hear what I had to say about it. When I spoke I found myself shouting, as one does to a foreigner, and in a kind of despair that he could not hear me. After the walk I would feel that I had worked off my duty and I was anxious to get him settled and reading in his Morris chair, so that I could go out and have a livelier time with other people. And he would sigh and look after me absentmindedly with perplexed loneliness.

For years afterward I have thought with real suffering about my father's loneliness. Such a wonderful man, and reaching out to me and wanting to know me! But he could not. He could not listen. But now I think that if only I had known as much about listening then as I do now, I could have bridged that chasm between us. To give an example:

Recently a man I had not seen for 20 years wrote me: "I have a family of mature children. So did your father. They never saw him. Not in the days he was alive. Not in the days he was the deep and admirable man we now both know he was. That is man's life. When next you see me, you'll just know everything. Just your father all over again, trying to reach through, back to the world of those he loves."

.Well, when I saw this man again, what had happened to him after 20 years? He was an unusually forceful man and had made a great deal of money. But he had lost his ability to listen. He talked rapidly and told wonderful stories and it was fascinating to hear them. But when I spoke—restlessness: "Just hand me that, will you?... Where is my pipe?" It was just a habit. He read countless books and was eager to take in ideas, but he just could not listen to people.

Well, this is what I did. I was more patient—I did not resist his non-listening talk as I did my father's. I listened and listened to him, not once pressing against him, even in thought, with my own self-assertion. I said to myself: "He has been under a driving pressure for years. His family has grown to resist his talk. But now, by listening, I will pull it all out of him. He must talk freely and on and on. When he has been really listened to enough, he will grow tranquil. He will begin to want to hear me."

And he did, after a few days. He began asking me questions. And presently I was saying gently:

"You see, it has become hard for you to listen."

He stopped dead and stared at me. And it was because I had listened with such complete, absorbed, uncritical sympathy, without one flaw of boredom or impatience, that he now believed and trusted me, although he did not know this.

"Now talk," he said. "Tell me about that. Tell me *all* about that."

Well, we walked back and forth across the lawn and I told him my ideas about it.

"You love your children, but probably don't let them in. Unless you listen, people are weazened in your presence: they become about a third of themselves. Unless you listen, you can't know anybody. Oh, you will know facts and what is in the newspapers and all of history, perhaps, but you will not know one single person. You know, I have come to think listening is love, that's what it really is."

Well, I don't think I would have written this article if my notions had not had such an extraordinary effect on this man. For he says they have changed his whole life. He wrote me that his children at once came closer; he was astonished to see what they are: how original, independent, courageous. His wife seemed really to care about him again, and they were actually talking about all kinds of things and making each other laugh.

Just as the tragedy of parents and children is not listening, so it is of husbands and wives. If they disagree they begin to shout louder and louder—if not actually, at least inwardly—hanging fiercely and deafly onto their own ideas, instead of listening and becoming quieter and quieter and more comprehending. But the most serious result of not listening is that worst thing in the world, boredom; for it is really the death of love. It seals people off from each other more than any other thing. I think that is why married people quarrel. It is to cut through the non-conduction and boredom. Because when feelings are hurt, they really begin to listen. At last their talk is a real exchange. But of course, they are just injuring their marriages forever.

Besides critical listening, there is another kind that is no good: passive, censorious listening. Sometimes husbands can be this kind of listener, a kind of ungenerous eavesdropper who mentally (or aloud) keeps saying as you talk: "Bunk...Bunk...Hokum."

Now, how to listen? It is harder than you think. I don't believe in critical listening, for that only puts a person in a straitjacket of hesitancy. He begins to choose his words solemnly or primly. His little inner fountain cannot spring. Critical listeners dry you up. But creative listeners are those who want you to be recklessly yourself, even at your very worst, even vituperative, bad-tempered. They are laughing and just delighted with any manifestation of yourself, bad or good. For true listeners know that if you are bad-tempered it does not mean that you are always so. They don't love you just when you are nice; they love all of you.

In order to learn to listen, here are some suggestions: Try to learn tranquility, to live in the present a part of the time every day. Sometimes say to yourself: "Now. What is happening now? This friend is talking. I am quiet. There is endless time. I hear it, every word."

Then suddenly you begin to hear not only what people are saying, but what they are trying to say, and you sense the whole truth about them. And you sense existence, not piecemeal, not this object and that, but as a translucent whole.

Then watch your self-assertiveness. And give it up. Try not to drink too many cocktails to give up that nervous pressure that feels like energy and wit but may be neither. And remember it is not enough just to *will* to listen to people. One must *really* listen. Only then does the magic begin.

Sometimes people cannot listen because they think that unless they are talking, they are socially of no account. There are those women with an old-fashioned ballroom training that insists there must be unceasing vivacity and gyrations of talk. But this is really a strain on people.

No. We should all know this: that listening, not talking, is the gifted and great role, and the imaginative role. And the true listener is much more beloved, magnetic than the talker, and he is more effective, and learns more and does more good. And so try listening. Listen to your wife, your husband, your father, your mother, your children, your friends; to those who love you and those who don't, to those who bore you, to your enemies. It will work a small miracle. And perhaps a great one.

❋ From Brenda Ueland's papers, the Minnesota Historical Society, courtesy the Schubert Club

✍ On Life ৯৺

I SIT HERE looking out the window. I have been working all night. I am wearing dark-blue flannel sailor pants, heavy brogues, a white cotton shirt, a red bow tie, a white sweatshirt washed so much that there are holes in it and the sleeves are frayed. I need a walk badly, for I have been working much too hard and steadily under pressure, for the last two months.

And it is queer, I have not a touch of resignation about the future, or nostalgia, or poetic mournfulness for the days that are gone. I seem to be entirely cheerful and full of anticipation. I seem to be always holding my breath with suspense, as though something wonderful were going to happen the next day and the next; and I wish everybody in the world could feel this way. And now goodbye.

❦ *Excerpted from* Me, *courtesy the Schubert Club, first published in 1939 by G. P. Putnam's Sons*

↭ *On Death* ↭

YOU KNOW much brighter souls than I—Blake, Swedenborg, and Jesus—great souls more pervious to the Invisible than I am, say that when we die we are not dead. I cannot help but believe that. It is a certitude. I cannot get away from the notion.

Death is unbearably tragic and grievous because it is a kind of farewell. But it is not forever. Those who are Yonder, in a queer way—I have discovered this myself—are more puissant than ever. They are more befriending, more strengthening, more helpful.

Then there is this thought. Rudolph Steiner, the Austrian mystic, said that the Catholic prayers for the dead are so right, so true, because the person who has died at first is a little lost. Our love helps him, makes it easier for him to find his way. I believe it.

❦ *From Brenda Ueland's papers, the Minnesota Historical Society, courtesy the Schubert Club*

APPENDIX

ᥬ Adventure ᥬ

*Fridtjof Nansen's Rectorial Address at St. Andrews University,
3rd November 1926.*

IN 1925 NANSEN WAS ELECTED HONORARY RECTOR
BY THE STUDENTS OF ST. ANDREWS UNIVERSITY. ON NOVEMBER 2ND,
1926, WHEN HE ARRIVED AT ST. ANDREWS STATION, HE WAS MET BY
A CROWD OF STUDENTS WHO BEDECKED THE TRAIN WITH A
POLAR BEAR DRESSED IN AN ACADEMIC GOWN AND CROWNED
WITH A MORTARBOARD. HE GAVE HIS SPEECH THE NEXT DAY.

SOLOMON IS SAID to have compared "the people unto the sea, and orators and counselors to the wind; for that the sea would be calm and quiet if the winds did not trouble it." If in the present case I may call you the sea, I am pretty sure that you are troubled enough already without the help of any orators. And yet, though I have never before felt any desire to cultivate windy oratory, I do wish I could be a tempest today, to do you credit.

But winds, whether strong or weak, may blow from so many quarters. I wonder what direction you expect me to blow from?

I have been wondering how on earth you ever came to think of making me your rector? Was it because long ago, long before you were born, I expect, a young fellow with the same name as mine made some journeys through the frozen North? You may have heard something about it when you were children. Or could it be because, during more recent years, my name has happened to be connected with several undertakings intended to alleviate the sufferings of unfortunate fellow

181

creatures?

I could not find out; and that was disheartening, as it might have given me my cue for this address, the delivery of which, I understand, will be my chief duty as your rector.

But after all, why should I worry? You will not remember what it was about anyhow.

You must not think that we old people are as self satisfied as we seem. We know well enough that although you are extraordinarily nice to us — sometimes at any rate — still, to be quite honest, you often think us intolerable bores with our heavy learning and good advice — at least I remember I did when I was your age — and not without reason perhaps.

Long ago La Rochefoucauld said that, "old folk like to give good precepts in order to console themselves for no longer being able to give bad examples." I do not know that we can altogether accept that definition, though there may be more truth in it than we realize at first.

I am sure, however, we shall all agree with the same sage, when he said that: "we never meet with any intelligent people but those who are of the same opinion as ourselves." As a rule, it is only by sad experience that we are enabled to verify the wisdom of opinions that differ from ours. How much easier life would be if we could be taught by others! But the real wisdom of life we have to discover with our own eyes.

"Experience doth take dreadfully high wages," your immortal Carlyle said, "but she teacheth like none other." Stick to that, young friends! Listen to authority and age; you may learn a great deal from those who are older than yourselves — but trust your own eyes still more, and keep them open. A truth acquired by the use of your own eyes, though imperfect, is worth ten truths told you by others, for besides increasing your knowledge, it has improved your capacity to see.

But although I believe that as strongly as any of you, here I stand, none-the-less, your rector, rather an old man, I am sorry to say, and I have to deliver an improving address to you who are setting sail on your voyage through life.

What shall I say? Well, I presume that a rectorial address should first say a few wise words about the ocean of life which you are to navigate. But I am afraid I can make you no wiser in that respect, the sea is so rough now, and the mist and scud so dense that it is difficult to see ahead.

A dangerous sea for the young to navigate, they say. I should think it would be a remarkably interesting voyage. One act of the play is finished — a new act is just beginning. There is ferment everywhere. Old established truths are overthrown; it is for you to find new ones.

Yes, indeed, the sea is difficult. Many may be wrecked, perhaps; but all the more will remain to be done by every one of you who has got the grit to do it. My friend Amundsen observed the other day that he was glad he was not born later, as then there would have been nothing left for him to explore except the moon. It made me think of Martin Frobisher who, 350 years ago, "resolved wyth himselfe to go... and to accomplyshe" the North West Passage "or bring true certificate of the truth, or else never to retourne againe, knowing this to be the onely thing of the worlde that was left yet undone, whereby a notable mind might be made famous and fortunate."

Now, it is not the aim and end of life to become "famous and fortunate." It is not so easy as that. You have come here to do your part and to do it well, wherever you are placed. And there have been many things worth doing since Frobisher's days, and there will be more than enough for you too, my friends. Let me speak of some of them.

We have heard much lately about the *decline* of *European civilization*; it has reached its old age, they say, and is on the way down hill. And amongst other things they point to the lack of originality and a certain alarming sterility in the productiveness of the West European brain nowadays, perhaps especially manifesting itself in the art of our time, and in the lack of commanding personalities.

But do not allow yourselves to become pessimists. This talk of decline is nothing new. Let us get it into true perspective. We like, of course, to think that mankind is constantly making progress; it is such a nice comforting idea. But is it right? Progress implies that we know whither we are going; and we can only advance towards a fixed point. But such a point is just what is lacking. You will remember that Archimedes long ago said, though in a different connection: "Give me a fixed point and I can lift the earth!"

Fancy if some of the ancient leaders of thought—Buddha, Socrates, Christ—came back to us, and we showed them all our marvelous inventions, and our scientific discoveries, the results of the great progress since their days. Would they not smile indulgently at us—as we smile at our children when they show us their favorite toys?

I imagine the following dialogue might have taken place between Socrates and Marconi:

Socrates, after having seen all the inventions, would say: "This is all very interesting, but what have you learnt about yourself?"

Marconi: "But do you not see what enormous importance it has for the whole of human life, for business, for economic conditions and development to be able to convey information quickly!"

Socrates: "But how has it helped *you*? Have you become a better man by it? And then if it helps some people, perhaps others suffer."

Marconi: "But look at the broadcasting which brings beautiful music and good lectures to thousands, and even to millions, of people!"

Socrates: "How, then, do these people get time for that which is infinitely more important, to *think for themselves?*"

No, we have no reason to boast ourselves better than our fathers. Indeed, it is more important than doubtful whether there is any proof of the superiority of the so called "civilized man" over his "uncivilized" ancestors. Let us go back some five or six thousand years to the ancient Egyptians, living in a Stone Age. When we see what those people accomplished with their implements, can we say honestly that we feel ourselves superior to them?

And if we go still further back—some twelve or fifteen thousand years—we find the Cro-Magnon people, a race certainly in no respect inferior to any of us. With a magnificent stature, taller than we are, perhaps six feet three inches in height, and what skulls! Look at the beautiful high arch of intelligence from the fine forehead to the neck! A cranium with one-sixth more brain than that of the modern European. Fancy if such a man had the education and knowledge of an undergraduate of our days, what could he not have made out of life if placed in our midst? He would certainly have done at least as well as any of us.

Oh no, my friends, let us be modest. The rising trend of evolution, which carried our ancestors from the level of the apes to that of the Cro-Magnon people, stopped thousands of years ago owing to the conditions of modern social life, especially to its urbanization, which interfere with the "survival of the fittest," and make the inferior elements of mankind the most prolific. The human race is certainly still changing and changing rapidly - but "it is no use galloping if you are going in the wrong direction."

These are questions of the gravest importance, to be earnestly studied by those of you who are going to be the reformers we await so anxiously.

But surely, even if the race may not have improved physically of late, our *ideas* have done so. Our *ethics* and *morality* have developed far beyond the primitive stage. Yes, certainly, so far as individuals go, though not to the extent that many people think, and certainly not when the individuals combine into groups.

Nations have hardly begun as yet to have real morality. They are little more than collections of beasts of prey. Private human virtues such as modesty, unselfishness, charity, love of one's neighbor, the feeling of solidarity, still strike them only too often as ridiculous folly if they are urged to practice them in their policies.

This may sound a harsh judgment, and perhaps it is too harsh. But let me give you an example that should have shocked much more profoundly than it did the public conscience of mankind. I mean the proceedings of the special Assembly of the League of Nations in March last.

Now, this League is just a great and remarkable adventure, a new ship sailing out along new tracks with the future hopes of mankind on board. It marks, we trust, the beginning of a new era in the world's

185

history, attempting as it does to introduce into the dealings between nations respect for those virtues I mentioned, and to create a feeling of solidarity, and establish real co-operation between them for the betterment of the world. We therefore expected much. But, alas! a new spirit of the world cannot be created in a day, and amongst the crew of that ship there are still many sailors who have not forgotten their old habits.

The nations of the world met in Geneva in March for one single purpose, which everyone believed to be not only desirable, but even essential to the future of Europe - the purpose of admitting Germany to the League. Everyone imagined that the way was clear. After the Locarno meetings, after the noble speeches breathing international brotherhood and love, we really thought that the nations of the world had at last turned over a new leaf. We may still hope, since the events of this September, that Locarno may have been the beginning of something new and better.

But in March many of our first bright hopes were tragically dispelled. Then we had the spectacle of one nation after another raising obstacles to the fulfillment of our common purpose, and doing so with a disregard for decency, which we had none of us believed it would be possible for them to show.

And in the end, as you remember, we had to leave Geneva defeated and dismayed, because some states were still determined to think solely of their own interests instead of the world at large.

Well, in September we repaired in part the disaster that had happened, and we are profoundly grateful for much that was said and done. But we remember, too, the foul, occult powers that were at work in March, and remembering them we cannot resist the conviction that there is something rotten outside Hamlet's State of Denmark.

Let me, however, give you another example: the Russian famine in 1921 - 22, when the Volga region and the most fertile parts of Russia were ravaged by a terrible drought — when something like thirty million people, or more, were starving and dying — dying by the thousand...

A heart-rending appeal for help went out to all the world, and eventually a great many people in this and in other countries helped, and helped generously. But many more were busy trying to find out first who was to blame. Was it the drought? Or was it the political system of the Russian State? As if that could ameliorate the terrible suffering or make any difference whatever to those who were dying of starvation!

But what was worse, there was in various trans-Atlantic countries such an abundance of maize at that time that the farmers did not know how to get rid of it before the new harvest, so they had to burn it as fuel in their railway engines. At the same time the ships in Europe were idle, and laid up, for there were no cargoes. Simultaneously there were thousands, nay millions, of unemployed. All this while thirty million people in the Volga region — not far away and easily reached by means of our ships — were allowed to starve and die, the politicians of the world at large, except in the United States, trying to find an excuse for doing nothing in the pretext that it was the Russians' own fault — a result of the Bolshevik system.

Fancy, if the unemployed had been put on board the idle ships, had been sent to South America, and had brought the maize to the Black Sea and saved the stricken millions, how much suffering they could have relieved. Do you not think that world would have been the better for it? I tell you that there is something rotten in the condition of the world. There is still ample scope for improvement.

The touchstone of real culture should be the feeling of solidarity. You, your family, your class, your nation, are only parts of the whole, passing links in space and time. But of that feeling there seems to be nothing as yet between nations, and mighty little between classes. In their relations you still have the morality of the savage who only considers his own advantage.

How strange that we have not yet outgrown these perpetual struggles and disputes between different classes of the same people about the division of the profit; that we have no more rational means of settling them than brute force: *strikes* and *lock-outs* — and that we use these weapons and stop working, even when there is unemployment and privation.

I often wonder what an inhabitant of some other globe would say if he could look down and see how we manage things upon this little planet of ours. Would he think that there were intelligent beings on this earth? Wasn't it Bernard Shaw who said some time ago that he did not know what the inhabitants of the other globes were doing, but he was firmly convinced that they used our earth as their lunatic asylum.

Yes, there can be no doubt that excessive nationalism as well as class warfare are dangers. But there may be dangers on the other side too. Let us not forget that national patriotism, as was mentioned by Lord Cecil in the last Assembly of the League, is a necessary stimulus for the development of the world.

Beware of the tendency towards too much internationalism, towards unification, towards creating a great uniform human family. Desirable as it might be in some respects I cannot help seeing a great danger in it. Increasing urbanization, uniform education, the rapidly improving means of transport and communication tend to abolish distance, and to wipe out those characteristic differences between peoples, nations, and cultures which have made life interesting and beautiful, and acted as an important stimulus to new thought.

There are several ideals in vogue nowadays, which, if realized, would lead us towards a dangerous monotony, a uniform grayness, in which it would be difficult to develop one's own personality.

All this may be difficult to alter, but we ought not to shut our eyes to it.

It is not very encouraging, the picture which your rector has drawn of the sea you have to navigate, of the stage on which you have to act your part in life. He has drawn it to the best of his knowledge, well aware that it is useless to paint with rosy colors when you will soon be caught in the gray mists of reality.

But you have the buoyant strength of youth, and when they tell you civilization is going down hill, remember it has been bad enough many times before in history. In spite of its age the world is young. And let us trust that we are in the spring when a new summer is born.

"April for me I choose;
In it the old things tumble,
In it things new refresh us;
It make a mighty rumble, —
But peace is not so precious
As that his will man shows.

......

In April the summer grows."
-Bjørnstjerne Bjørnson
(TRANSLATED BY A.H.PALMER)

What we call development goes in great waves up and down. If you are in the trough you have always the possibility of rising in to a crest ahead of you. The great thing in human life is not so much where we stand as in what direction we are moving. And, mind you, it is not the stage that makes your actions great or small. It is for you yourselves to create your role on the stage.

"Men at some time are masters of their fates,
The fault, dear Brutus, is not in our stars
But in ourselves, that we are underlings."

If the world is out of joint it is for you to put it right, to make it a better place to live in, each of you to the best of his ability. As I told you, there is ample scope for improvement.

The old beaten tracks do not take us to our goal. It is time to begin prospecting in new lands. We need you, young friends, with fresh eyes capable of seeing the simple elemental things - ready to try new trails, to run risks, and dare the unknown.

My distinguished predecessors, Barrie and Kipling, have spoken to you about *courage* and about *independence*, two heaven born qualities for this voyage of life, and never more needed than in our day. They are worth infinitely more than all your wireless, and broadcasting, and all

189

the rest. But a third genius is needed to complete the group of deities - it is the *spirit of adventure*. It is about this genius that I wish to say a few words to you today.

Who is she? No less than the spirit that urges mankind forward on the way towards knowledge. The soul's mysterious impulse to fill the void spaces, analogous to Nature's *horror vacui*.

Don't you remember how, as a child, when some part of the house was closed, and vaguely suspected of being haunted, you felt fearfully frightened - and yet pined to get in there to meet those mysterious ghosts? The risks added to the charm. And one day when you were alone, you somehow managed to get in. But how disappointed you were when you saw no ghosts after all! That was your awakening spirit of adventure. It is in every one of us. It is our mysterious longing to do things, to fill life with something more than our daily walk from home to office, and from the office back home again.

It is our perpetual yearning to overcome difficulties and dangers, to see the hidden things, to penetrate into the regions outside our beaten track — it is the *call of the unknown* — the longing for the Land of Beyond, the divine force deeply rooted in the soul of man which drove the first hunters out into new regions — the mainspring perhaps of our greatest actions — of winged human thought knowing no bounds to its freedom.

We will find in the lives of men who have done anything, of those whom we call great men, that it is this spirit of adventure, the call of the unknown, that has lured and urged them along their course.

Kipling says in *Kim*: "God causes men to be born... who have a lust to go abroad at the risk of their lives and discover news — today it may be of far off things — tomorrow of some hidden mountain — and the next day of some near by men who have done a foolishness against the State. These souls are very few, and of these few not more than ten are of the best." But, my young friends, though modesty is a becoming virtue, let us always believe that we are amongst those ten!

For most of us ordinary people life is a voyage from harbor to harbor, along a fairly safe coast. We run no great risks. There are plenty of shoals and sunken rocks, no doubt; but we have reliable charts and sailing directions, and if anything unforeseen should happen, we can always put in for the night at the nearest port. On the whole a fairly comfortable and not very exciting existence. But what about the things worth doing, the achievements, the *aims* to live and die for?

No, although many of us have to do it, coastal navigation is not really to the liking of our race. Our ancestors, yours and mine - the Norsemen - they did not hug the coast. With their undaunted spirit of adventure they hoisted their sails for distant shores, and no fear of risks could keep them back, the call of the unknown summoned them across the seas, and it was *they* who led the way across the oceans. If it had not been for that spirit of adventure, how differently history would read today – and in my opinion the difference would not be for the better.

Let me tell you an example of the awakening spirit of adventure in the history of the British Empire - how it led on the one hand to disaster, but on the other to greatness.

In the middle of the sixteenth century England's power on the sea was very modest. We hear, for instance, that in 1540 London had, with the exception of the royal fleet, only four vessels of more than 120 tons burden. Then awoke the idea that it might be possible to find a short route to the riches of Cathay or China, north of Norway and Russia. This seemed a promising adventure. The merchants of London, a society named "The Mystery and Company of the Merchant Adventurers," equipped three ships, and placed the expedition under the command of the gallant general Sir Hugh Willoughby, on account "of his tall, handsome appearance, and of his rare qualities as a soldier."

The ships sailed in May 1553, amid great expectations and much rejoicing. Willoughby with two ships and sixty-two men had to winter on the coast of the Kola Peninsula, and when Russian fishermen came to the place next spring they found two ships with only dead men on board. They had all died of scurvy. When the two ships were subsequently sailed homeward, one of them was wrecked on the coast of Norway and the new crew lost, the other, with 24 men on board, disappeared and was never heard of again.

Such was the unlucky fate of those two ships in spite of their names, *Bona Esperanza* and *Bona Confidentia*. But the third vessel, *Edward Bonaventure*, under command of the able Richard Chancellor, was separated from the two other ships in a gale north of Norway, and arrived at Vardö. Here Chancellor evidently heard about the route to the White Sea and the trade between the Norwegians and the Russians. This was a new adventure, and as the other ships never came, he decided to try that route.

He met, however, with some Scotsmen, who do not seem to have been as enterprising as Scotsmen are supposed to be. They warned him earnestly against the voyage, but he sailed all the same, "determining," as he declared, "either to bring that to pass which was intended, or else to die the death." They came into the White Sea and to the river Dvina. Chancellor went to Moscow and was well received by the Russian Czar, Ivan the Terrible. Next summer he returned in his ship to England, bearing a letter from the Czar.

This voyage and the so-called discovery of this Old Norse route to Russia through the White Sea form an important turning point in the development of English commerce and shipping.

It meant the opening of a great new market for English goods. A profitable trade with Russia developed quickly, and the *Muscovy Company*, which received special privileges, became so rich and powerful that it could soon support important undertakings in other parts of the world as well. A rapid development of the English mercantile marine followed.

Thus it came about that England was soon in a position to compete with the stronger sea powers even in other regions.

This episode, in fact, marks the beginning of Great Britain's power on the sea. The story shows how apparently small accidents may prove decisive in the history of a whole people... If it had not been for the true spirit of adventure in that one man, Richard Chancellor... England's important trade with Russia would not have commenced at that time, the development of her shipping would have been very different, and the history of the world would have proceeded along other lines.

I am convinced that the future development of the possibilities of your own people, as well as of those of mankind, will depend on some of you young people striking boldly out along new tracks. I am sure that the great events in the world depend on the spirit of adventure shown by certain individuals in grasping opportunities when they occur.

And so it is in the personal life of every one of us. Let me tell you a little about myself, not because that self is a personage of any great importance, or a good example; but simply because it is the only one I have. And we must all of us judge life from the standpoint of our own experience.

Now, when I look back on my own life, it strikes me that if anything worth doing has ever been accomplished on that crooked course of regrettable irregularities, it was only due to a certain spirit of adventure, acting, however, in a sporadic and imperfect way.

In his admirable address, Barrie proposed that a good subject for his successor's rectorial address would be: "the mess the rector himself has made of life." Little did he know how much to the point that subject would be for your present rector. Barrie warned you against M'Connachie, his imaginary other half, who is always flying around on one wing, dragging him with him. And what shall we other poor mortals say, whose M'Connachies do not write charming plays for us, like Barrie's, but merely lead us astray?

How many nasty tricks that unruly fellow has played me! When we were young, and plodding steadily along a fairly promising road, he would suddenly bolt up some unexpected sidetrack, and I had to follow and make the best of it.

Now, do not mistake that fanciful creature for the spirit of adventure. Far from it, he is just Master Irresponsible — an emotional, impulsive, and quarrelsome person, who is very easily bored, and thinks it extremely dull when you go on with the same thing for long, and who, therefore, is always on the look-out for something new to turn up, like a child looking round for new things to play with.

But the spirit of adventure may still save the situation and see you through, once you have been diverted on to a new trail. For its nature is not to want continually to change; on the contrary it is to want to see the end of things. And once you have embarked upon an undertaking, the spirit of adventure will not give in — whether you sink or swim — till the work is done and done well.

Do not think that adventure is child's play, or that the heights can be won in a day. You wish to rise and be great; but remember:

> "*The heights by great men reached and kept,*
> *Were not attained by sudden flight,*
> *But they, while their companions slept,*
> *Were toiling upwards in the night.*"
> —HENRY WADSWORTH LONGFELLOW

Real greatness was *never* attained without patience and industry. "Genius is an inexhaustible power of taking trouble," Carlyle said. "Patience is power," adds an Eastern proverb, "with time and patience the mulberry leaf becomes satin."

Check Master Irresponsible then, and consider well before you move. Make your preparations carefully; they can never be too careful – the road is long. No guess-work, no approximations. But when you strike out, then throw your whole self into the enterprise. Set all your sails. No wavering, for "self-trust is the first secret of success" – don't check your boat when you are tacking.

We pass many crossroads on our way through life, and the test of a man is how he behaves at each crossroad. Some people cannot decide, they waver, wishing to keep all ways open, and always looking back they end up getting nowhere. The traveler of the right mettle may consider well, but then he takes one road and sticks to that; and he always arrives somewhere. For him the only road is then the road ahead of him, and there is no way back.

I have always thought that the much-praised '*line of retreat*' is a snare for people who wish to reach their goal.

Let me tell you one secret of such so called successes as there may have been in my life, and here I believe I give you really good advice. It was to burn my boats and demolish the bridges behind me. Then one loses no time in looking behind, when one should have quite enough to do in looking ahead — then there is no choice for you or your men but *forward*. You have to do or die!

Let me try to tell you how it worked in my case. I have to apologize once more for devoting so much time to myself; but I see no way of avoiding that, if I am really to tell you something about life. I was an undergraduate once, even younger than most of you, probably, and a "ne'er-do-well" except for some little sport, perhaps. According to Carlyle, "the first of all problems for a man to find out is what kind of work he is to do in this universe." But even this little problem I had not been able to solve.

I had a leaning to science; but to which science? Physics and Chemistry interested me the most; but Master Irresponsible — over whom I had no control at the time — did not like that kind of life much. One day he suddenly took it into his head that Zoology would be better, as that promised more fun — more shooting and out of door life. Consequently we went in for Zoology.

Then one day, the irresponsible creature suddenly suggested that we should go on a voyage to the Arctic Sea, under the pretext of studying the animal life of the polar regions. I was 20 then — and off we went! That was the first fatal step that led me astray from the quiet life of science.

It gave me more Arctic sport, more interest in various polar problems than actual zoological research, and on that voyage we were caught and beset in the pack ice, and drifted for over three weeks towards the then unknown east coast of Greenland. I saw the mountains and glaciers, and a longing awoke in me, and vague plans revolved in my mind of exploring the unknown interior of that mysterious, ice-covered land. I returned home. I was made Curator of the Zoological Museum at Bergen. The Arctic dreams were more or less forgotten. I went in, body and soul, for Zoology, and especially for microscopical Anatomy. For six years I lived in a microscope. It was an entirely new world, and Master Irresponsible kept fairly quiet during those years, and we were well on the way to become a promising young zoologist.

During that period, too, I visited this university, just forty years ago this autumn, and met for the first time your great zoologist, my old friend Professor McIntosh, who is still amongst us. While I was Curator in Bergen I was visited by a young Scottish zoologist, my friend D'Arcy Thompson, who is now one of your professors.

I wrote some works, especially on the microscopical anatomy of the nervous system. They contained some discoveries of value, I believe, but still more important were perhaps the new problems which they raised. We were full of ambitious plans for new investigations to solve those problems. Most of those investigations have later been made by others, but some of the problems are still waiting to be solved, I believe.

Anyhow, we had possibilities of doing work worth doing, and of becoming a sound man of science and a university professor. I still feel a pang of regret when I think of those lost opportunities.

But just then Master Irresponsible took advantage of a weak moment, and played me one of his most fatal tricks. We had just finished a treatise on the nervous system, with the result that the author's own nervous system was overstrained and needed a little rest. Then he brought back the Arctic dreams and told me that the time had come to carry out our old plan of crossing Greenland. It would not take that long, and we could soon return to the nervous system again with renewed vigor. He would not have succeeded if he had not been joined by a stronger ally, the spirit of adventure. To resist those two together was hopeless, I had to go!

Many attempts had been made to cross Greenland, the unknown interior of which was supposed to be covered by an enormous ice cap, called the Inland Ice. But all these attempts had been made from the inhabited west coast and had not succeeded. How, then, was my plan formed?

It was one autumn evening in Bergen, in 1883. I was sitting and listening indifferently as the day's paper was being read by my friend the clergyman [Pastor Wilhelm Holdt]. But suddenly my attention

196

was roused by a telegram: Nordenskiöld had come back from his expedition towards the interior of Greenland; he had had two Lapps with him, who had found good snow for skiing, and had covered incredible distances on ski. In that same moment it struck me that an expedition of Norwegian ski-runners, going in the opposite direction, from east to west, will cross Greenland. The plan was ready.

My idea was this, that if one started as previous expeditions had done, from the west side, one would have the "flesh pots of Egypt" behind one, and in front the unexplored desert of ice and the east coast, which is little better. So it struck me that the only sure road to success was to force a passage through the floe belt, land on the desolate east coast of Greenland, and thence cross through the unknown over to the inhabited west coast. In this way one would burn one's boats behind one; there would be no need to urge one's men on, as the east coast would attract no one back, while in front would lie the colonies on the west coast with the allurments and amenities of civilization.

The plan when it was published was declared by the so-called "competent authorities" to be utterly impossible. One of them, a Dane, who had traveled along the ice bound east coast of Greenland, where I proposed to land, declared in a public lecture that the plan "betrayed absolute ignorance of the true conditions" and showed "such absolute recklessness that it was scarcely possible to criticize it seriously." I dare say he was right in his way. Some authorities criticized especially the unpardonable rashness of destroying the bridges behind you. The first thought of a good general and leader was always to secure a safe line of retreat, without which his men would not go on with confidence.

But I had always thought "the line of retreat" a wretched invention, as I told you before. And I was justified by the events. In spite of my youthful ignorance and lack of experience, and although our preparations and equipment were lamentably imperfect in several respects—as my companion Captain Sverdrup, here present, would tell you if he were to give you his candid opinion—the expedition was carried out in accordance with the plan. The method worked out extremely well, the lack of the line of retreat simplified matters and acted as a stimulus, making up for the defects in our preparations.

The same method was also used for our next expedition. Of course, having once really set foot on the Arctic trail, and heard the "call of the wild," the call of "the unknown regions," we could not return to the microscope and the histology of the nervous system again, much as I longed to do so.

I had conceived an idea that there was a continuous drift of the ice across the unknown regions round the North Pole, from the sea north of Bering Straits and Siberia on into the sea between Greenland and Spitzbergen. I found more and more proof, which definitely convinced me of the existence of such a drift. Then it struck me that this drift of the ice could be used for the transport of an expedition across the unknown regions. It would only mean building a ship of a special shape, sufficiently strong to resist the ice pressure, and this ship we could push as far as possible into the pack ice on the side where it was drifting northwards, let her be frozen in, and then the ice would carry us across the regions which the previous expeditions had tried in vain to reach. It simply meant working with the forces of nature instead of against them. Here again the same principle was applied. Once we were well started on this expedition, there would be no line of retreat. Our hope was ahead of us, and so the ship was called the *Fram*, which means *Forward*.

When this plan was published it was severely attacked by most of the very first authorities on polar exploration in Great Britain and in other countries. As the prominent Arctic navigator, Admiral Sir George Nares, expressed it: It totally disregarded the adopted Arctic axioms for successfully navigating an icy region, which were, "that it is absolutely necessary to keep close to a coast line, and that the farther we advance from civilization, the more desirable it is to insure a reasonably safe line of retreat." He did not believe in a drift of the polar ice as assumed by me.

That splendid Arctic explorer, Admiral Sir Leopold M'Clintock, said that it was impossible to build a ship strong enough to resist the ice pressure in the winter, and he believed, as did the majority of the others, that there was no probability of ever seeing the *Fram* again when once she had given herself over to the pitiless polar ice.

The ship was built. Her famous builder with the Scottish name, Colin Archer, was a Norwegian whose father had come from this country. The expedition was carried out in full accordance with the plan. We had a great deal more knowledge and more experience this time. The drift of the ice was found to be very nearly what was expected, and the ship was strong enough to resist even the most desperate attacks of the ice. We went into the pack ice north of the New Siberian Islands in 1893, and the ship came out of the ice again north of Spitzbergen three years later, safe and sound, after having drifted across the unknown regions.

But the spirit of adventure is always urging you on, once you begin to listen to it. When we had drifted with the *Fram* for a long time, we saw that she would drift across, and the end of the expedition would be attained.

But then the adventurous spirit found out that something more could be done by two of us leaving the ship with dogs and sledges. We could travel across the drift ice towards the Pole, and in that way explore parts of the unknown regions outside the drift route of the *Fram*. But in that case we could not think of returning to the drifting ship, as we should not know where she had drifted to in the meantime. We should have to go to Franz Josef Land and Spitzbergen where we might find a sealing vessel to bring us home. Again we had to break the line of retreat, and again the method worked well.

Hjalmar Johansen went with me and, while the *Fram* and the rest of the expedition were left in the safe hands of Captain Sverdrup, we set off from the ship with dogs and sledges on 14th March 1895.

We expected our sledge expedition to last three months at most, and carried food for that period. But the ice was more difficult than we expected. At last we reached the north coast of a land which afterwards turned out to be Franz Josef Land, but it was so late in the season that we could not get through, so we had to winter. Instead of the three months we were provisioned for, we had to live through fifteen months before we met with people.

We built a stone hut, we shot bears, and walrus, and for ten months we tasted nothing but bear meat. The hides of the walrus we used for the roof of our hut, and the blubber for fuel. In the following summer we quite unexpectedly met British people, the Jackson-Harmsworth Expedition, on the south coast, and came home in their ship.

I tell you all this just to make you understand how things that might seem impossible can be done when you have to do them, and how a life you may think hard is easily lived when you have a goal to work for. You may think it was hard to live a long winter dug in, and on nothing but bear meat; but I can assure you it was a happy time, for we had the spring and the home coming to look forward to.

You may notice that in the case of these plans, as also on many occasions later in life, I had the misfortune to have most of the competent authorities of the world against me, declaring my views and my plans to be impossible. However, I had the advantage of living a great deal alone in my life, and had thus acquired the habit of making up my mind without asking the opinion of others.

It has obvious advantages to stand alone; it makes you more independent in your action, and you are less apt to be misled by others. Ibsen said that man is strongest who stands most alone.

But this does not imply that every man who stands alone is strong, or that every plan which competent people declare to be impossible should be attempted. Beware of obstinacy and fool-hardiness! For a strong man there is a great danger in resistance and contradiction. It takes a superior man to allow himself to be convinced in the heat of argument by the logic of another.

I think it was Montaigne who wondered whether the fanaticism which is created by unflinching defiance of the judge's violence and of danger, has not more than once made a man persist, even to the stake, in an opinion for which — among friends and in freedom — he would not have singed his little finger. There is the spirit of adventure, but the reverse of the medal.

You have to take risks, and cannot allow yourself to be frightened by them when you are convinced that you are following the right course. Nothing worth having in life is ever attained without taking risks. But they should be in reasonable proportion to the results which you hope to attain by your enterprise, and should not merely depend on luck, giving your ability to overcome the risks no chance of coming into play. Even an animal may have that kind of foolhardiness; and success can give you no real satisfaction if it depends on mere accident.

Let me tell you a case where, in my opinion, the risks should not have been taken. It was the ill-fated expedition of the prominent Swede Andrée. He had formed a project of crossing the unknown North Polar regions in a balloon. It was in 1896, before the days of dirigibles. He hoped to be able to keep the balloon up during the time required for the winds to carry it across the unknown regions.

He went to Spitzbergen in 1896, intending to start from there in his balloon, *Örnen* (i.e. the Eagle). He did not, however, think the meteorological conditions sufficiently favorable for a start that summer. He therefore returned and postponed his start till the following year.

In the meantime we came back from our expedition in the *Fram*, across the unknown North Polar Sea, and our meteorological observations collected during three years in those regions were naturally of great interest to Andrée. At his request I sent him a full extract of them when he was again on his way north to Spitzbergen in the early summer of 1897. I also sent him a letter in which I pointed out that, as he would see, the prevailing winds and the meteorological conditions during the summer months would not as a rule be favorable to his undertaking. And I expressed the hope that, as he had once had the courage to return when he saw that the conditions were unfavorable, he would be able to show the same courage again.

He wrote back from Trömso, thanked me for the documents and my kind advice, but declared that he would not be able to show that courage a second time.

On 11th July 1897, the noble Swede and his two gallant companions started on their flight from Spitzbergen into the unknown. They never returned.

This was certainly the noble spirit of adventure, which did not shrink back before risks. We cannot but admire it, but we profoundly regret that those splendid qualities could not have been used for a better purpose.

Why do I give you these examples from the life of exploration and adventure? Because all of us are explorers in life, whatever trail we follow. Because it is the explorers with the true spirit of adventure we now need if humanity shall really overcome the present difficulties, and find the right course across that dangerous sea ahead of us which I mentioned at the beginning of this address. You will all find your adventure, for life itself is an adventure.

But try not to waste your time in doing things which you know can be done equally well by others. Everyone should try to hit upon his own trail. Do not lose your opportunities, and do not allow yourselves to be carried away by the superficial rush and scramble, which is modern life.

The first great thing is to find yourself, and for that you need solitude and contemplation, at least sometimes. I tell you deliverance will not come from the rushing, noisy centers of civilization. It will come from the lonely places! The great reformers in history have come from the wilderness.

My friend Knud Rasmussen – whom we regret not to have amongst us today – told me a remarkable story about a medicine man or conjurer of the primitive Eskimo of the Barren Grounds in northern Canada. I should like, for your benefit, to repeat it here. This simple savage, who had hardly ever seen a white man, said to his friend and colleague, Rasmussen: "The true wisdom is only found far from men, out in the great solitude, and can only be attained through suffering. Privation and suffering are the only road to wisdom, and they alone can open a man's mind for that which is hidden to others."

I think these words... show more understanding of the secret of wisdom than you will find in a great many people in our countries. He went on to describe how, in order to become a sage, i.e., a medicine man or conjurer, a man has to fast for fourteen days in an unheated snow hut at the coldest time in the middle of winter. Then comes another medicine man with a drink of hot water and a little raw meat. And after that the man has to go on fasting again as long as he possibly can. He should never finish his struggle for wisdom; but most people are satisfied too soon, and that is the reason why there is so little wisdom in the world.

This is the true spirit of adventure, which must always press on. It makes one think of these lines of Tennyson:

> "This gray spirit yearning in desire
> To follow knowledge like a sinking star,
> Beyond the utmost bound of human thought."

These are questions well worth thinking over; but I tell you there are many people who do not get time even to think over what they themselves hold to be the purpose of their lives. What is the purpose of yours? Are you all of you certain you have the answer ready?

Are you out for happiness? Well, many people are. But believe me, my friends, you need not look for it. The great thing is to do your best, and to be independent of all other "necessities." Dear me, how perfectly unnecessary many of these "necessities' really are.

> "And if through chance of circumstance
> We have to go barefoot, sir,
> We'll not repine - a friend of mine
> Has got no feet to boot, sir.
>
> This Happiness a habit is
> And Life is what we make it:
> See! there's the trail to Sunnydale!
> Up, friend! and let us take it."
> —"To Sunnydale," from Rhymes of a Rolling Stone
> by Robert W. Service

Are you poor? What luck. No time lost in looking after your belongings. There is always so much trouble with property. And you cannot really be poor on this earth. Let me tell you what our great poet Wergeland once said:

> "Have I no heaven because it is full of drifting clouds,
> fairylands of the sun?...
> Complain not under the stars of the lack of bright spots in your life!
> Ha! are they not twinkling
> as if they would speak to you?
> How Venus sparkles tonight!
> Have the heavens also Spring?...
> What riches for a mortal!"

My dear young friends, let me give you one warning based on long and sad experience. Do not let your flight be clogged by all those trifles which are now considered necessities of life. Mind, by making your baggage train longer, you clip your wings.

Oh youth, youth! what a glorious word! Unknown realms lie ahead of you, hidden behind the mists of the morning. As you move on, new islands appear, mountain summits shoot up through the clearing mists, one behind another, waiting for you to climb; dense new forests unfold for you to explore; free boundless plains for you to traverse. You are "foot loose and heart free" to sail beyond the sunset and to roam the universe.

What a joyous thing to see day dawning and to know that you are bound on a voyage to new realms. "Your soul bounds upward on beams of light to the vault of heaven."

You laugh at the risks and smile at the dangers, youth's buoyant faith and self-trust is in command. The storm cannot reach you.

And lo! far ahead, above the mist and the scud, rise your Land of Beyond! We all have a Land of Beyond to seek in life — what more can we ask? Our part is to find the trail that leads to it. A long trail, a hard trail, maybe; but the call comes to us, and we have to go.

Rooted deep in the nature of every one of us is the spirit of adventure, the call of the wild — vibrating under all our actions, making life deeper and higher and nobler.

> *"Have you known the Great White Silence?...*
> *Have you broken trail on snowshoes? mushed your*
> *huskies up the river,*
> *Dared the unknown, led the way, and clutched the prize?...*
> *Have you suffered, starved and triumphed, grovelled down, yet grasped*
> *at glory,*
> *Grown bigger in the bigness of the whole?*
> *'Done things' just for doing, letting babblers tell the story..*
> *Have you seen...*
> *The simple things, the true things, the silent men who do things-*
> *Then listen to the Wild - it's calling you.*
>
> *Let us probe the silent places, let us seek what luck betide us;*
> *Let us journey to a lonely land I know.*
> *There's a whisper on the night wind, there's a star agleam to guide us,*
> *And the Wild is calling, calling... let us go."*
> — "CALL OF THE WILD" BY ROBERT W. SERVICE

AUTHORS' BIOS

PER EGIL HEGGE (FOREWORD) is a one of Norway's best-known journalists. He was an editor, columnist and cultural commentator for many years at Aftenposten, Oslo's largest newspaper. He served as its correspondent in Moscow from 1969 to 1971, and in Washington, D.C. from 1977 to 1981. He is the author of several books, including biographies of Fridtjof Nansen and King Harald V of Norway. He chaired the Norwegian branch of PEN-International from 1985 to 1988. In 2003 he was decorated with the Royal Norwegian Order of St. Olav (Knight 1st Class).

ERIC UTNE (INTRODUCTION, and Editor) is an entrepreneur, publisher and educator. In 1984 he founded Utne Reader magazine, a "field guide to the emerging culture," which he edited and published for 15 years. He now writes a back-page column in every issue. Utne is a member of the executive committee of the Nobel Peace Prize Forum and of the advisory boards of Ecotrust and the World Future Council. He has a B.E.D. (Environmental Design) from the University of Minnesota and serves as a Senior Fellow at the University's Center for Spirituality & Healing. Utne is the step-grandson of Brenda Ueland. He lives in Minneapolis.

ATTENTION LIBRARIANS, RESEARCHERS AND COLLECTORS

A special, unabridged and unexpurgated edition of *Brenda, My Darling* is available for purchase to qualified parties. The edition includes passages deleted from the abridged edition due to sexual content, reproductions of several of Nansen's handwritten letters and six full-length nude self-portraits that Nansen sent to Ueland. The photos are for research, collecting and curatorial purposes only, and are not for reproduction or distribution by any means. They are strictly protected by US and international copyright law.

Send inquires, including qualifications and credentials, to:

Ueland/Nansen Initiative
c/o Utne Institute
4259 Linden Hills Blvd.
Minneapolis, MN 55410, USA
Or visit: www.utneinstitute.org

ACKNOWLEDGMENTS

Thanks to my beloved **Susan Lyon** for teaching me about love, "soul resonance," and Lyon's Law. Her constructive criticism, creative suggestions,and indelible fingerprints are all over this book.

Thanks to Brenda's daughter **Gaby Ueland McIver** and Brenda's dear friend and benefactor **Bruce Carlson** for their original blessings and encouragement for this project. Thanks to the **Minnesota Historical Society** for preserving Brenda's papers and to **Kathleen van Bergen** and **The Schubert Club** for permission to publish them.

Special thanks to Professor **Geir Lundestad**, Director, Norwegian Nobel Institute, whose early and consistent encouragement helped me decide to publish this book. **Steinar Bryn,** Ph.D., Professor at the Nansen Humanistic Academy and leader of its Dialogue Project; **Carl Emil Vogt,** Ph.D., historian at the University of Oslo and author of a forthcoming book on Nansen's international and humanitarian work from 1920-1930; and **Roland Huntford**, author of the 2001 biography, *Nansen: The Explorer as Hero*, played similar roles. A half dozen others gave similar encouragement and support, but asked to remain anonymous.

Thanks to **Mary Fiorenza** for sharing with me her research and Ph.D. thesis, *Methods & Models of Writing & Living: Composing Brenda Ueland's Writing Life*; and to **Vigdis Devik** for sharing her Master's thesis, *Privileged Family – Privileged Ethnicity: Ethnic Parental Polarization and Historical Contexts that Shaped the Life of Norwegian-American Columnist Brenda Ueland.*

Thanks to **Karin Berg**, author of *Nansen and His Women*, for her early assistance and encouragement, and to **Fredrik Kjus** and **Anita Helland** for helping me appreciate the breadth and depth of Fridtjof Nansen's accomplishments and legacy, and for their gracious hospitality.

Thanks to **Danielle Maestretti** for transcribing Nansen's letters, to **Theresa Wolner** for her expert indexing, and to **Samantha Grosz** and **Bernadette Miller** for their thoughtful critiques and suggestions, and editorial help with the manuscript.

Thanks to **Thomas R. Smith** for his help in naming this book, and to **Jim Lenfestey** for editing my labored prose, making it far more interesting than it would otherwise be.

Thanks to **Craig & Patricia Neal**, **Paul Strickland**, **Ned Holle**, **Tove Borgendale**, **John & Kerry Miller**, **Linda Bergh**, and **Jennifer Fox**, and to the **Linden Hills Elders**, the **Saturday Morning Walkers**, and **The Outliers**, whose faithful friendship and wise counsel sustain me.

ACKNOWLEDGEMENTS

Thanks to **Nina Rothschild Utne** for critiquing drafts of the Introduction, and for teaching me so much about the tendance of the soul and the crucible of life.

Thanks to my sons **Leif, Sam, Oliver, and Eli Utne** for making my life so endlessly fascinating and fun, and for teaching me so much about parenting and friendship.

Thanks to my niece, **Emily Utne**, the brilliant and gifted graphic designer who designed this book. Her father (my brother Tom) was my best friend and favorite person to work with. Collaborating with Emily on this book has been déjà vu. I felt Tom's presence, and pride in her throughout.

Thanks to **Cathy** and **Bob Utne** for their empathetic insights and challenging questions.

Thanks to **Bob O'Brien** for loving my sister **Mary** so emphatically and so well, and for his thoughtful critique of the manuscript.

Thanks to **Gene Gollogly, Sabine Weeke, Elizabeth Jarrett Andrew, Sharon Franquemont, The Dialogos Group, Richard Leider, Kjell Berg**, Ambassador **Ben Whitney, Dag Hareide, Inge Eidswaag** and **Hans Tarjei Skaare** for their wise counsel and helpful introductions. Thanks to sculptor **Kirsten Kokkin** for suggesting I talk with Orfeus. Thanks to **Hal W. Johnson** and **Tracey Thompson** for their "reckless generosity." Thanks to **Claes Lykke Ragner,** of the Nansen Institute for his tour of Nansen's home, Polhøgda.

Thanks to **Anne Melgård**, Curator of the Manuscripts Collection of Norway's National Library, for her meticulous review and annotations of the letters. Thanks to **Marit Greve** for her magnanimous blessings. Thanks to **Ole Rikard Høisæther, Cato Schiotz, Heidi Lesniak,** and **Vesna Bryn,** for their gracious hospitality. Thanks to **Ingunn Henriksen** and **Ellen Sue Ewald** for trying so hard, and to **Anne-Mette Høisæther** for the exquisitely designed ring.

Special thanks to **Mathias Bolt Lesniak** for leaping into this project without hesitation and helping me navigate the unfamiliar waters of Norwegian book publishing.

And finally, this book would not be possible without the love that **Brenda Ueland** and **Fridtjof Nansen** had for each other. I bow to them, and thank them, for the evidence of their love that they left behind.

ILLUSTRATION CREDITS

Page x, "Leaping Woman," by Fridtjof Nansen, Owner: The Schubert Club

Page 28, Photographer: Unknown; Owner: National Library of Norway

Fridtjof Nansen photo section
Page I: Photographer: A. Mostue; Owner: National Library of Norway (www.nb.no)
Page II: Photographer: Unknown; Owner: UN High Commission on Refugees (UNHCR)
Page III (top): Photographer: Fridtjof Nansen; (bottom): Photographer: Unknown; Owner of both: National Library of Norway
Page IV (top): Photographer: John van der Fehr; Owner: National Library of Norway; (lower left and right): Photographer: Unknown; Owner: UNHCR, (both)
Page V: Photographer: Unknown; Owner: National Library of Norway
Pages VI & vii: Photographer: Fridtjof Nansen; Owner: Minnesota Historical Society (MHS)
Page VIII: Photographer: Unknown; Owner: UNHCR

Page 124, Photographer: Unknown; Owner: Eric Utne

Brenda Ueland photo section
Page IX: Photographer: G.W. Murdock; Owner: Minnesota Historical Society (MHS)
Page X: Photographer: Unknown; Owner: Minneapolis Star and Tribune (MTS)
Page XI (top): Photographer: Unknown; Owner: MHS; (bottom): Photographer: Unknown; Owner: MST)
Page XII: Photographer: Unknown; Owner: MST
Page XIII (top): Photographer: Unknown; Owner: MHS; (lower right): Photographer: Unknown; Owner: MHS; (lower left): Photographer: Unknown; Owner: MHS
Page XIV (left): Photographer: Eugene G. Garrett; Owner: MHS; (right): Photographer: Unknown; Owner: MST
Page XV: Photographer: Unknown; Owner: MHS
Page XVI (upper left): Photographer: Unknown; Owner: MHS; (upper right): Photographer: Unknown; Owner: MHS; (bottom): Photographer: Bob McClure; Owner: Eric Utne

INDEX

May 23rd, evening.

Oh Brenda, my darling, my girl, my mistress, my everything! I had written the letter and was going to mail it, when yours of May 10th arrived this evening and I must open the envelope again and add these few lines, will write more soon. Oh, happiness, it is as if I had you here in my arms, and felt your lovely body pressed close to mine. You are a sorceress, indeed, you have tied me hand and foot, soul and body, everything I am lost. I remember well before I had seen you, I was curious to know what you would be like, and whether perhaps there might be awaiting some nice acquaintance. When after dinner with your sister I spoke to you about meeting, and touched your hand and you pressed mine just so much that I thought I could feel it, and you proposed that I might come to Stamford, I thought that perhaps it might develop into some more